Essential Histories

The Irish Civil War 1922–23

Essential Histories

The Irish Civil War 1922–23

Peter Cottrell

First published in Great Britain in 2008 by Osprey Publishing,
Midland House, West Way, Botley, Oxford OX2 0PH, UK
443 Park Avenue South, New York, NY 10016, USA
E-mail: info@ospreypublishing.com

A CIP catalogue record for this book is available from the
British Library

ISBN: 978 1 84603 270 7

Page layout by: Myriam Bell Design, France
Index by Alan Thatcher
Typeset in GillSans and 1 Stone seriff
Maps by The Map Studio
Originated by PDQ Digital Media Solutions Ltd, Bungay, UK
Printed in China through Bookbuilders

08 09 10 11 12   10 9 8 7 6 5 4 3 2 1

For a catalogue of all books published by Osprey Military and
Aviation please contact:

NORTH AMERICA
Osprey Direct, c/o Random House Distribution Center,
400 Hahn Road, Westminster, MD 21157
E-mail: info@ospreydirect.com

ALL OTHER REGIONS
Osprey Direct UK, P.O. Box 140 Wellingborough, Northants,
NN8 2FA, UK
E-mail: info@ospreydirect.co.uk

Osprey Publishing is supporting the Woodland Trust, the UK's
leading woodland conservation charity, by funding the dedication
of trees.

www.ospreypublishing.com

Author's Note
Throughout this book, I have used the term 'Republican'
to describe the anti-Treaty forces, because the Free State
Provisional Government supported the treaty that retained
the monarchy and fell short of the Republic envisaged in
the 1916 declaration. The Free State leaders and the majority
of their supporters may well have been republicans, but it
was not for this cause that they were fighting in 1922–23.

Dedication
My wife Heather

Acknowledgements
I would like to thank Donal Buckley, Seán Connolly, Seán Dunne,
Cormac Doyle, Peter McGoldrick and Kevin Myers for all their
help and encouragement.

Editor's Note
All images credited to George Morrison are courtesy of:
The Irish Civil War by Tim Pat Coogan and George Morrison,
published by Weidenfeld and Nicolson, an imprint of the
Orion Publishing Group, London.
© Tim Pat Coogan and George Morrison 1998

Contents

Introduction

On 6 December 1921 a treaty was signed between the representatives of the British Government and the self-proclaimed Irish Republic, which brought to an end the cycle of violence that has become known as the Anglo-Irish War, Irish War of Independence or more colloquially as 'The Troubles'.[1] Although the terms of the Anglo-Irish Treaty fell far short of the Independent Irish Republic that many members of the Irish Republican Army (IRA) had fought for since the Easter Rising of 1916, it did grant the majority of Ireland Dominion[2] status within the Empire, placing it on a par with Australia, Canada, New Zealand and South Africa.

The new Irish Dominion, known as the Irish Free State, or Saorstát Éireann in Irish, may have enjoyed greater autonomy from Whitehall than envisaged in the abortive 1914 Irish Home Rule Act, but the fact that six Ulster counties of what is now known as Northern Ireland were to remain within the United Kingdom made the peace unacceptable to many IRA men. The treaty was also rejected by many of the rebellion's political leaders. Despite the fact that Èamon de Valera, in his capacity as President of the Irish Republic, issued a telegram on 7 October 1921

1. See Essential Histories 65, *The Anglo-Irish War: The Troubles of 1913–22* (Oxford: Osprey Publishing, 2006) for further information.
2. The terms of the Treaty, as signed, covered the whole of Ireland, although Northern Ireland (recently created under the Government of Ireland Act) was granted the option of withdrawing from the Anglo-Irish Treaty and remaining under the direct rule of Westminster.

Dublin, July 1922: During the occupation of the Four Courts the IRA did nothing to prevent National Army troops from building extensive barricades around their positions. This position on O'Connell Street is typical of National Army fire positions. © Hulton-Getty Library

Minister of Defence Richard Mulcahy, formerly Chief of Staff, presenting the Republican colours to Captain O'Daly. Standing to the left of Mulcahy in civilian attire is Kevin O'Duffy, the new Chief of Staff. (Corbis)

authorizing the Irish delegates 'to negotiate and conclude' a treaty with the British, he was ultimately to lead the opposition to it.

The struggle for Irish independence from Britain had unified the entire spectrum of Nationalist sympathies, from those who sought political reform to those who supported armed insurrection; however, the Treaty now destroyed what unity there was. Consequently, the IRA followed the tradition highlighted by the Irish writer and IRA member Brendan Behan (1923–64) who once quipped that the first thing on the agenda at an IRA meeting was 'the Split', and turned on itself in an internecine conflict that surpassed the Anglo-Irish War in bitterness and divided the Irish political landscape for the rest of the 20th century.

To some Nationalists the landslide victory of the Irish Republican party Sinn Féin in the 1918 General Election was clear evidence that the Irish electorate supported both armed rebellion and Irish independence. In reality such a victory was possible only because the

old Irish Parliamentary Party (IPP) had collapsed after failing to deliver Home Rule or limited devolution for Ireland in modern terms, whilst Sinn Féin also cut a deal with the Irish Labour Party that involved not contesting seats fielding Sinn Féin candidates. Consequently, it is likely that many voted Sinn Féin for want of an alternative.

When the Treaty was put to the Irish electorate on 16 June 1922 they overwhelmingly supported it. Of the 128 seats in the Dáil – the Irish Parliament created by Sinn Féin after the 1918 General Election – 92 went to pro-Treaty candidates; thus the anti-Treaty Republicans who took up arms against the first independent Irish state since 1801 had no electoral mandate and consequently lacked the popular support enjoyed by the IRA during the Anglo-Irish War. This vote can be interpreted as either

The Four Courts battle in Dublin. The ruins of buildings in O'Connell Street, being searched by members of the St John's Ambulance Brigade for bodies of the wounded and dead. An excellent idea of the damage wrought during the fighting is given in this photo. (Corbis)

a general 'war-weariness' after nine years of hostility and two years of direct conflict or quite simply an indication that the bulk of the Irish electorate was not as wedded to 'the Republic' as Èamon de Valera liked to believe.

Some of the Treaty's supporters, including IRA leaders Michael Collins and Richard Mulcahy, were committed Republicans but accepted the Treaty as the best that they could achieve at the time. Collins famously argued that the Treaty was a stepping-stone, giving Ireland 'the freedom to achieve freedom'. He was well aware that although the IRA had not been defeated by the British they had not won either and that a renewal of hostilities would bring no guarantee of victory.

The British ruthlessly exploited this fear and constantly threatened to renew military action if the Treaty was rejected. Winston Churchill even showed Collins a draft call-out notice authorizing that 'the Army Reserve (including the Militia) be called out on permanent service' to renew hostilities in Ireland if the negotiations failed. For the British the issue was that Ireland should remain within the orbit of the British Empire under the Crown, as an independent Republic was unacceptable to them. Even de Valera recognized the legitimacy of Britain's strategic concerns on its Atlantic flank and sought 'association' with the Commonwealth rather than membership of it.

According to Professor Michael Hopkinson it is 'impossible to come to other than negative and depressing conclusions about the war and its consequences'.[3] Unlike many civil wars, Ireland's was relatively brief, large areas of the country witnessed little or no fighting and conventional military operations of any significant scale were over by September 1922. Yet in 1948 the Irish judge Kingsmill Moore commented that, 'Even now Irish politics is largely dominated by the bitterness of the hunters and the hunted of 1922.'

No accurate figures exist regarding casualties, although Saorstát records refer to

3. Michael Hopkinson, *Green against Green, The Irish Civil War* (Dublin: Gill and Macmillan Ltd, 1988)

The Provinces of Ireland

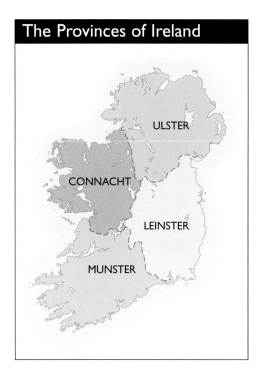

ULSTER

CONNACHT

LEINSTER

MUNSTER

800 members of its National Army (NA) dying between January 1922 and April 1924. Historians J.M. Curran and R. Fanning mention 4,000–5,000 combined NA/IRA military deaths but Hopkinson assesses these figures as too high. Although all three agree that more people died during the Irish Civil War than had been killed during the Anglo-Irish War no one knows exactly how many civilians became victims.

What is apparent is that it was a bitter contest. By the time the Republican forces 'dumped arms' in the summer of 1923 over 12,000 people had been interned by the Saorstát, 77 Irregulars executed in reprisals and dozens of others murdered whilst the war had cost Ireland from £17m–30m. According to Frank Aiken, who became IRA Chief of Staff in April 1923, 'War with the foreigner brings to the fore all that is best and noblest in a nation – civil war all that is mean and base.'

The war also took a heavy toll on those who had led Ireland's revolution. Harry Boland, Cathal Brugha, Erskine Childers, Michael Collins, Liam Lynch and Liam Mellows were but a few of those who died

violently whilst Arthur Griffith died of a brain haemorrhage. Mulcahy blamed de Valera for the civil war and was never allowed to forget his own part in the subsequent executions policy, whilst in 1927 the IRA murdered Saorstát Minister of External Affairs Kevin O'Higgins in revenge for his role in the civil war, sparking fears of a renewal of hostilities. For many years the de Valera and O'Higgins families lived within yards of each other in the Dublin suburb of Blackrock, yet might as well have been on different planets.

Like all civil wars, Ireland's was a bitter experience for the country. It pitted brother against brother, quite literally in the case of Cork IRA officers Tom and Seán Hales, and did much to define the physical and political geography of modern Ireland. Modern Ireland's major political parties Fianna Fáil and Fine Gael have their roots in the conflict and the British-backed Saorstát's victory ensured *de facto* and later *de jure* recognition, by the Irish State, of Northern Ireland's continued membership of the United Kingdom.

After its defeat in 1923 the subversion of Northern Ireland became the main *raison d'être* of the Republican movement although it is often forgotten that it views the Irish State as equally illegitimate, refusing for many years to participate in its constitutional politics for fear of investing it with legitimacy. Even a casual flick through Eunan O'Halpin's 1999 book *Defending Ireland – The Irish State and its Enemies since 1922* (Oxford: Oxford University Press) highlights how much of Ireland's security forces have been focused on containing the IRA.

The fact that in the early 1970s Republican activist Bernadette Devlin could sneeringly refer to the Republic of Ireland as 'Charlie Haughey's Free State', although 'Free State' had been abandoned as a title in 1937 when it was renamed Éire and all references to the British monarchy were expunged from its constitution, is a good illustration of this attitude. Part of the impetus for this change was, in the Irish Government's own words, that 'there continued to exist throughout the country a substantial body of opposition to it owing to its being circumscribed by the terms of the Treaty'.

In an article published in the *Cork Examiner* on 23 February 2000, Ryle Dwyer stated that 'as a people [the Irish] we have been largely ignorant of our history and have thus allowed ourselves to become virtual prisoners of these emotions'. The civil war was a period of history that was studiously avoided in Irish schools until well into the 1960s and Dwyer could not remember it ever being mentioned during his school days. This is why perhaps the emotional divisions of the civil war persist without being fully understood.

This article, entitled 'Turning a Blind Eye to the Casualties of our Civil War', also observed that although Fine Gael and Fianna Fáil have never really 'been divided by ideology', both having common roots in Sinn Féin, 'but by those irrational emotions which led to the Civil War', the then Fine Gael leader John Bruton TD (*Teachta Dála*: deputy to the Dáil) ruled out any possibility of a coalition with Fianna Fáil, confirming that Moore's observation was as valid in 2000 as it had been in 1948.

According to Hopkinson the Irish Civil War had a depressing effect on the international community's perception of the new state that conformed to every negative stereotype of the Irish. The owner of the *Manchester Guardian* commented that, 'who would have believed that, having got rid of us, the Irish would start a terror of their own?' More importantly the lack of a clear-cut victory and failure to come to terms with the war's consequences played a major role in determining how the population of the 26 counties viewed their own state as well as its immediate neighbours.

Both the Anglo-Irish War and the Irish Civil War were about who had the right to govern Ireland and what form that government should take. Arguably both conflicts were also as much about tensions between central and regional authority as between the differing Irish political and cultural traditions whilst the continued ignorance surrounding them allows many myths and prejudices to perpetuate.

Despite the change of regime, the legacy of the RIC was evident in Ireland's new police force. (Image courtesy of the National Library of Ireland)

Chronology

1918 **14 December** Sinn Féin wins a landslide victory in the Irish General Election

1919 **21 January** Traditional start date of the Anglo-Irish War

1921 **11 July** Anglo-Irish War ends
6 December A treaty is signed but is denounced by de Valera because it recognizes the Crown. The Irish Republican Brotherhood (IRB) calls for unity and the Dáil votes in favour of the Treaty. The IRA's General Headquarters (GHQ) splits nine to four in favour of the Treaty

1922 **January** De Valera resigns as President of the Dáil and is replaced by Arthur Griffith. Collins is appointed chairman of the Executive Committee of the Provisional Government. British rule ends on 16 January when NA troops take over Dublin Castle
February IRA in Co. Limerick reject the authority of the Provisional Government
March A standoff develops between NA and anti-Treaty IRA in Limerick. The Dáil prohibits the IRA Convention planned for 26 March. Mulcahy orders the suspension of IRA officers who attended the Army Convention. The Army Convention rejects the authority of both the Provisional Government and GHQ
April The Army Convention elects a new 16-man Executive. Liam Lynch is elected IRA Chief of Staff
13 April Anti-Treaty IRA under Rory O'Connor occupy the Four Courts, Dublin, the centre of Irish justice
May Fighting breaks out in Kilkenny. The planned IRA offensive in Northern Ireland fails. Collins and de Valera make their electoral pact. The British suspend troop withdrawals from Southern Ireland leaving 5,000 men in Dublin. The Northern Ireland Government bans all Republican organizations
16 June Pro-Treaty candidates win 78 per cent of the seats in the General Election
22 June The IRA assassinate Unionist MP Field Marshal Sir Henry Wilson in London. The British Government blames the anti-Treatyites. The Provisional Government is given an ultimatum by the British Government to deal with the rebels. NA surrounds the Four Courts
28 June–5 July The civil war begins. The Four Courts are captured but fighting spills over onto O'Connell Street, killing 65, wounding 281 and causing £3m–4m of damage. Cathal Brugha is amongst the dead. Lynch establishes his GHQ in Limerick
July The Provisional Government establishes a War Council chaired by Cosgrave, and Collins becomes NA Commander in Chief. IRA prisoners are offered parole if they undertake not to fight against the Saorstát. Despite setbacks in Co. Cork NA troops capture Blessington (Co. Dublin) and the towns of Kilkenny, Waterford, Limerick and Tipperary. Kilmallock (Co. Limerick), is captured by anti-Treaty forces. Co. Mayo is also overrun after an NA amphibious landing
August NA amphibious landings in south-west Munster secure key towns in Co. Kerry, Co. Limerick and Co. Cork. The IRA abandon conventional operations and commence a guerrilla

campaign. Griffith dies and is replaced by Cosgrave

22 August Collins is killed in an ambush in Co. Cork

September The Southern Irish Parliament, created by the 1920 Government of Ireland Act, sits and merges with the Dáil. Anti-Treaty TDs create an alternative 'Republican' government. The Dáil passes the Public Safety Act

October The Provisional Government offers an amnesty to IRA who surrender by 15 October. The Army Emergency Powers Act and the Saorstát Éireann Constitution come into force

November On 17 November the first executions under the Public Safety Act take place. Lynch establishes an HQ in Dublin and orders the assassination of all TDs who voted for the Public Safety Act as well as high court judges and hostile newspaper publishers. Erskine Childers is arrested by NA troops, court-martialled and executed on 24 November. Further executions of IRA follow and Emmet Dalton resigns from the NA

December The British Acts creating the Saorstát and its constitution are given the royal assent and ratified by the Dáil, bringing Saorstát Éireann into being. Tim Healy becomes Governor-General, Cosgrave becomes President of the Executive, Lord Glenarvy becomes Chairman of the Senate and all TDs take the oath of allegiance to the Crown. Northern Ireland votes itself out of the Saorstát. The 'Neutral' IRA is formed

Looking down O'Connell Street over O'Connell Bridge, the area where hot fighting was witnessed. Crowds of Dubliners gathered to watch the fighting in Dublin in July 1922. (Corbis)

Motorised National Army patrols faced many of the same problems as the British - bad roads and an indifferent civilian population concealing enemy guerrillas. (Image courtesy of the National Library of Ireland)

7 December Pro-Treaty TD Major-General Seán Hales is assassinated outside the Irish Parliament building, Leinster House

8 December Rory O'Connor, Liam Mellows, Joe McKelvey and Dick Barrett are executed. The executions are illegal but no further TDs are killed. The NA executes nine more IRA under the Public Safety Act

1923 January The NA executes 30 IRA and captures Liam Deasy. Paddy Daly takes command of NA in Co. Kerry. The houses of 37 senators are burned out in the first two months of 1923. The 'Old' IRA is formed

February Lynch orders reprisals if NA executions continue. The Irish Government offers another amnesty. Liam Deasy and IRA prisoners in Limerick, Cork and Clonmel gaols appeal for an end to the war. Lynch and other senior anti-Treatyites remain more optimistic. Both sides reject the Neutral IRA's call for a truce

March Captive IRA members are blown up in Ballyseedy, Killarney and Caherciveen, Co. Kerry and 26 others are shot. The anti-Treaty Executive narrowly votes to continue the struggle. The Irish Government decides to place the NA under civilian control and establishes a Supreme Army Council to 'exercise a general supervision and direction of strategy'

April NA achieves a high degree of success in Co. Mayo. Austin Stack and Dan Breen are captured and 13 IRA executed. Lynch is killed in a skirmish and is replaced as IRA Chief of Staff by Frank Aiken

27 April The anti-Treaty leadership decide to suspend offensive operations (though orders to cease fighting were not issued until 14 May). Over 12,000 IRA are in captivity

May The Irish Government rejects de Valera's peace terms. Two IRA are executed in Ennis, Co. Clare

24 May Aiken orders the IRA to dump arms. De Valera tells Republicans that 'further sacrifice ... would now be in vain ... Military victory must be allowed to rest for the moment with those who have destroyed the Republic.' The civil war is over. Michael Murphy and Joseph O'Rourke are the last IRA members to be executed, on 30 May

The Anglo-Irish War

In many respects the Irish Civil War bore remarkable similarities to the conflicts that had rent Ireland during the previous 200 years, in that it was fought between Irishmen with different views of how their country should be governed. Its principal difference was that it was contested over how an independent Irish State should be governed, though the nature of that state's relationship with its British neighbour was also central to the cause of the war, as was the existence of Northern Ireland.

British influence had dominated Irish politics for centuries and in 1801 Ireland been absorbed into the United Kingdom by an Act of Union passed by the Irish Parliament. Ireland was always the junior partner in the Union, and efforts to break the link by both revolutionary and constitutional means culminated in a war of independence that finally removed the British from 26 of Ireland's 32 counties in 1922.

The Anglo-Irish War of 1913–22 bore many of the hallmarks of a civil war, especially in Ulster, and the Irish Civil War of 1922–23 was to a great degree the endgame of that conflict. The IRA campaign had effectively undermined the rule of law in rural areas and legitimized political violence. The problem that the Saorstát faced was that a significant number of the IRA objected to the Treaty that had established it, even if the majority of the Irish electorate did not, and felt that they were morally justified to overthrow it.

Although Ireland was never isolated from events in Britain, it was in the 12th century that the island was drawn into the orbit of the English and later the British Crown. The relationship between Ireland and its neighbour was often fraught but it was not until 1798 that an Irish insurrection aimed to break with the British Crown and create a secular republic along Franco-American lines. Rather than severing the link, the failure of the United Irishmen drew Ireland formally into the United Kingdom.

Despite this, the United Irishmen were the spiritual ancestors of the modern Irish Republican movement and provided the inspiration for every subsequent Irish rebellion. It would, however, take 120 years before political violence was able to change the Anglo-Irish relationship. For the bulk of the 19th century it was constitutional rather than revolutionary Nationalism that proved to be the driving force in Irish politics.

The 1829 Catholic Emancipation Act gave political rights to Catholics across the United Kingdom. Of course, as 80 per cent of the Irish were Catholics this had a significant impact on the Protestant-dominated political and economic landscape of Ireland. By 1921 land reform and emancipation ensured that Catholics were sharing in the prosperity of the country and owned over 400,000 of Ireland's 470,000 smallholdings.

Between 1882 and 1918 the Irish Parliamentary Party (IPP) under the leadership of Charles Stuart Parnell and later John Redmond was the face of Irish Nationalism in the British Parliament and held the vast majority of Irish seats. It was moderately effective in promoting Irish issues such as land reform and Home Rule. By disrupting and frustrating Parliament's business it was able to force a weak Liberal Government to pass a Home Rule Bill in 1913.

The 1913 Home Rule Bill was the third to be put before Parliament and effectively offered Ireland a devolved parliament in Dublin with limited powers similar to that established in Scotland in 1998 rather than independence. Even this was too much for

Irish Unionists, who feared a Catholic-dominated government in Dublin. In Ulster, especially, opposition was particularly fierce and the Protestant majority there established the Ulster Volunteer Force (UVF) to resist Home Rule by force if necessary.

The Nationalists formed the National Volunteers in response and by 1914 two armed camps existed in Ireland with radically opposite aspirations. The scene was set for civil war. To make matters worse the preponderance of Irish Protestants in the British Army's officer corps brought into question its impartiality. In March 1914 Brigadier-General Sir Hubert Gough, the commander of the cavalry brigade based at the Curragh, Co. Kildare, and 57 of his officers threatened to resign if ordered to impose Home Rule on Unionists by force.

Fortunately for the Government the 'Curragh Mutiny' was overtaken by events and the outbreak of World War I defused the crisis. It also gave the Government the opportunity to postpone Royal Assent to the Home Rule Bill until after the war. Postponement of Home Rule split the Nationalists and although the majority of National Volunteers followed Redmond's advice and fought for king and country, a small splinter group, the Irish Volunteers, remained at home planning to overthrow British rule.

Unlike the wider National Volunteer movement the Irish Volunteers, led by Èoin MacNeill, were Republican revolutionaries and thoroughly infiltrated by the Irish Republican Brotherhood (IRB). Created in the 1850s the IRB had strong links with the Irish-American community and was a secret society dedicated to throwing off the 'yoke of Saxon tyranny' and creating an Irish Republic. IRB members under the direction of Patrick Pearse, Tom Clarke and Séan MacDermott, who sat on the IRB's supreme council, held most of the key positions in the Irish Volunteers.

On Easter Monday, 24 April 1916, roughly 1,000 Irish Volunteers and the socialist Irish Citizens' Army led by Pearse and his colleagues seized the General Post Office, the Four Courts and several other locations around Dublin. A week later the Easter Rising had been crushed and its leaders imprisoned. Although British intelligence reports had known a rising was being planned it came as a bolt from the blue for most Dubliners. The fighting devastated the city centre and hostile crowds jeered Volunteers as they were led away into captivity.

The British response to the Rising was predictable, if a little ill advised. The proclamation of an Irish Republic and praise for their 'gallant [German] allies in Europe' at the height of World War I was anathema to the British and many Irish who had relatives fighting their 'gallant allies'. The army, under the provisions of the Defence of the Realm Act (DORA), court-martialled and shot 15 of the rebels as traitors.

Irish MPs protested against the executions and the Government's apparent lack of control over the army. The shootings turned the leaders into Nationalist martyrs and did much to turn the Easter Rising from a military failure to a spiritual victory. In the gesture politics of Irish Republicanism it proved to be a tour de force and created an emotional response amongst the Irish, and in the words of W.B. Yeats, 'A terrible beauty is born'.

The death of Redmond in March 1918 accelerated the decline of the IPP and its failure to prevent conscription being extended to Ireland further undermined the appeal. Although its new leader, John Dillon MP, had condemned the executions after the Easter Rising, his party had backed the British war effort and over 200,000 Irishmen had joined the colours between 1914 and 1918. The majority were Nationalist but many became convinced that only the Unionist minority would be rewarded and Britain would renege on its commitment to Home Rule.

The party that benefited most from the declining fortunes of the IPP was Sinn Féin, which sought to portray itself as the authentic voice of Irish Nationalism. Sinn Féin, meaning 'ourselves alone' in Irish, had been founded in 1905 by an Anglophobic Irish journalist of Welsh extraction named Arthur Griffith. Sinn Féin had originally envisaged a 'dual monarchy' solution to the 'Irish Question' along Austro-Hungarian lines.

The personal links between Sinn Féin and participants in the failed Easter Rising were so close that many erroneously referred to it as the Sinn Féin Revolt and its supporters as Sinn Féiners. In reality Sinn Féin had played no part in the 1916 Rising but by 1917 it had become thoroughly infiltrated by militant Republicans. This perception was reinforced when the only leading rebel of 1916 not to be executed, Èamon de Valera, was elected its President.

De Valera, a US citizen of Irish-Hispanic stock, was to become the public face of Irish Republicanism and in many respects went on to dominate Irish politics until his death in 1975. De Valera was a consummate politician and David Lloyd George once commented that dealing with him was like trying to pick up mercury with a fork.

Perhaps because of his American connections, de Valera was conscious that the battle for Irish independence was a trans-Atlantic affair and made every effort to court favour in the United States. Irish-America was a source of funding and arms through organizations like Clan na Gael as well as a refuge from the British for men 'on the run', and men like Co. Tyrone-born Joseph McGarrity and veteran Fenian John Devoy worked hard to publicize the cause in America.

By 1918 Sinn Féin had become thoroughly Republican in its outlook and argued that the British Parliament had no jurisdiction over Ireland. Consequently when the British called a General Election in December 1918 Sinn Féin announced that although they would stand in the elections

General Richard Mulcahy (centre) flanked by two senior National Army officers. Mulcahy made his name during the 1916 Rising and became Chief of Staff (COS) of the Volunteers. He was appointed COS of the National Army and became CinC after Collins' death. He was also Minister of Defence and held responsible by many Republicans for the executions of IRA prisoners. (Image courtesy of Donal MacCarron)

successful candidates would not take their seats in Westminster.

When the results were in, Sinn Féin had won 73 of Ireland's 105 seats. Republicans took this as a mandate for creating a Republic but the result was not as simple as it first appears. In December 1910 the IPP had taken 83 seats, the Unionists 19 and the Liberals one, whilst Sinn Féin had none. Although the electorate had been increased by the extension of the franchise in 1918, many of those who voted Sinn Féin would probably have voted IPP in earlier elections.

In 1918 only six IPP candidates were returned. In addition the Unionist vote increased from 19 to 26 MPs. The Labour Party had done a deal with Sinn Féin and agreed not to contest seats with a Sinn Féin candidate, which effectively meant that no Labour MPs were elected. Labour had obviously expected some sort of *quid pro quo* but was bitterly disappointed when Sinn Féin took power.

Although the 1918 General Election was in effect a landslide victory for Sinn Féin it is an oversimplification to say that the bulk of the Irish electorate had transformed from constitutional Nationalists to militant Republicans between 1910 and 1918. For many, voting Sinn Féin was the only alternative to voting Unionist and was probably as much a protest vote against Anglo-Irish policy as it was an endorsement of an Irish revolution.

Regardless of the nuances, the Republican movement interpreted the result as a mandate for a war against the British and on 21 January 1919 two events took place that perhaps symbolize the beginning of that conflict. In the Mansion House, Dublin the first *Dáil Éireann* met to form an 'independent' Irish government and at Soloheadbeg, Co. Tipperary a party of IRA under the command of Seán Treacy carried out the first of a series of deliberate attacks on the British Government's representatives in the community, the Royal Irish Constabulary (RIC).

The Dáil, whose members are known as *Teachta Dála* (TD) or deputies to the Dáil, elected de Valera President of the Dáil and for the next two and a half years acted as Ireland's underground government. The military campaign was directed not by Cathal Brugha, the Minister of Defence, but by the Minister of Finance and Director of Intelligence, Michael Collins. Collins, an ex-Post Office clerk and 1916 veteran from Co. Cork, proved to be an excellent organizer and adept intriguer. Under his direction the IRA waged a ruthless guerrilla war against the agents of the British Crown.

In December 1920 the British Parliament passed the Government of Ireland Act, sometimes called the 4th Home Rule Act, in an attempt to end their Irish troubles. The Act provided for a Southern Irish Parliament in Dublin and a Northern Irish Parliament in Belfast to govern the Protestant North. From the start Ulster's Protestants had wanted to remain part of the United Kingdom and were determined to make sure that if they were given an unasked for parliament they would make sure that it prevented any sort of union with the Southern State.

The partition of Ireland into two entities enshrined in the Government of Ireland Act was never intended to be permanent and the British hoped that Ulster would opt into the Saorstát at some date in the future. De Valera and other Republicans objected to the division and saw it as yet another example of 'perfidious Albion's' divide and rule policy. It never crossed the mind of de Valera or many other Republicans, past and present, that Unionists could genuinely desire to be both Irish and members of the UK.

To Republicans the Unionists were at best misguided Irishmen being manipulated by the British and at worst 'foreign' Planters (Anglo-Scots colonists) who had stolen their land from the 'native' Irish. It did not help that the majority of Unionists were Protestants and so a sectarian fault ine divided them from the Republicans they despised. However, not all of the men who fought to preserve the Union were Protestants, conversely, not all those who fought to establish a Republic were Catholics, and the vast majority of policemen killed by the IRA were Irish Catholics.

The Anglo-Irish War was bitterly contested and degenerated into a cycle of terror and counter-terror as combatants on both sides carried out illegal killings. Both sides argued that they were legally and morally justified in their actions but ultimately the inability of either side to defeat the other brought about a truce in the summer of 1921. The truce was effectively the end of the war and led to the treaty negotiations that resulted in the creation of Saorstát Éireann.

In the solution to one conflict, however, lay the seeds of the next. The IRA had fought for a Republic and what they had been given was partition and Dominion status within the British Empire. Many felt a palpable sense of betrayal when the Irish electorate

Kevin O'Higgins TD, Sinn Féin activist during the Anglo-Irish War and Provisional Government Minister for Home Affairs. He was a bitter enemy of the anti-Treaty Republicans and a fierce critic of the National Army's conduct of military and policing operations. The IRA assassinated him in 1927. (Corbis)

voted overwhelmingly to accept the Treaty and believed that only a continuation of the armed struggle would achieve the Republic that so many had died for. Collins had known that the Treaty would divide the Republican movement but had gambled that a flawed peace was preferable to a renewal of violence on a scale hitherto unseen in Ireland. It was a gamble that would cost him his life.

The combatants

The military forces on both sides in the civil war had their roots in the IRA. The pro-Treaty forces became the NA and the anti-Treaty element continued to refer to itself as the IRA even though the Irish and British Governments and press called them Irregulars. For convenience the opposing forces are referred to as the NA and IRA.

Republican forces

The anti-Treaty IRA had its roots in the IRA that had fought the British during the Anglo-Irish War, and used that title and its rank structures throughout the Irish Civil War. The majority of IRA units that had fought against the British declared against the Treaty and the Republicans utilized the existing IRA battalion, brigade and divisional structures of the Anglo-Irish War.

Although the Irregulars adopted the IRA's organization they did not inherit many of its key personnel or indeed equipment. Nor did they enjoy the same levels of popular support seen by the IRA during the Anglo-Irish War. When West Cork IRA leader and ex-British soldier Tom Barry was on the run in the winter of 1922 he admitted that he had to be careful not to fall into 'the wrong hands' as the majority of the population were hostile to the Republicans.

When the Dáil accepted the Treaty it split the Republican movement. When the majority of IRA GHQ Staff, including Collins, backed the Treaty, Rory O'Connor, Liam Mellows, Sean Russell and Seamus O'Donovan walked out. In March 1922 Liam Forde, Officer Commanding (OC) Mid-

IRA irregulars man a barricade on the Leitrim–Sligo border, July 24, 1922. Their lack of uniforms and equipment was fairly typical of rebel forces in the civil war. (Corbis)

Limerick IRA Brigade, declared that he no longer recognized GHQ's authority, and a banned IRA Army Convention voted that the organization 'shall be maintained as the Army of the Irish Republic under an Executive appointed by the Convention'.

Liam Lynch was elected head of the Executive and eventually became IRA Chief of Staff until he was killed on 10 April 1923, when he was replaced by Frank Aiken from Armagh. Just as the Dáil had exercised little control over the IRA during the Anglo-Irish War the Republican 'Government' had little control over it during the civil war. Despite his nominal position as President of the Irish Republic de Valera was marginalized and Republican policy was so disjointed that in July 1922 Lynch's Assistant Chief of Staff Ernie O'Malley asked him to 'give me an outline of your military and national policy as we are in the dark here with regard to both'.

The IRA had three major difficulties to overcome if they were to win. Firstly they needed safe areas to operate in, secondly they required arms and thirdly they needed money. South-west Ireland was the heartland of anti-Treaty resistance until an NA

ABOVE The Provisional Government having been duly installed, an Irish Republican Army volunteer stands sentry at the entrance to Dublin City Hall. (Corbis)

BELOW September 1922: an Irish Air Force gunner practises his aim from the back seat of a biplane during the Irish Civil War. © Hulton-Getty Library

The Dublin Guards on parade, 1922. (Corbis)

offensive in August 1922 deprived them of this key ground. Ironically some areas that had played little or no part in the rebellion against the British became hotbeds of IRA activity.

In Northern Ireland and Britain the split threw the IRA into disarray and allowed the British to keep them firmly under control. In addition the Saorstát sent undercover teams into these areas to keep tabs on them. Some British and Northern IRA units did participate in the civil war but deprived of coherent direction their activities were limited.

In June 1922 the IRA had some 6,780 rifles to equip 12,900 men. Throughout the war they never broke their dependence upon arms captured from the NA although they did try and supplement this by smuggling guns from overseas. To do this they needed money and in the spring of 1922 over 650 armed robberies took place on the IRA Executive's orders with almost £50,000 being stolen on 1 May 1922 alone.

Initially they attempted to decapitate the Provisional Government, which had been created by the Treaty to administer the Free State until a general election could be held, by seizing key points in central Dublin. Instead they managed to replicate the failures of the Easter Rising but without gaining the sympathy vote that the Rising had elicited. Between July and August 1922 they attempted to defeat the NA in the field but this strategy failed and they reverted to the methods used during the Anglo-Irish War, forming small flying columns and active service units.

Although effective their attacks on the railway network led de Valera to complain that if they continued 'the people will begin to treat us like bandits'. Assassinations and arson did nothing to further their cause and simply prompted a wave of reprisals and executions by the Saorstát that overshadowed anything done by the British.

By May 1923 the military situation was hopeless; outgunned by the NA Aiken ordered his men to dump their arms and wait until 'our time will come' – *Tioclaidh ar la*. De Valera was also consigned to the political wilderness until 1932, when he became the first Fianna Fáil *Taoiseach* (Prime Minister).

Saorstát Éireann forces

The legal basis for the NA was the Defence Forces Temporary Provisions Act passed on 3 August 1923. Its creation was retrospectively dated to 21 January 1922 when its first unit, the Dublin Guards, was formed. It was known in Irish as *Oglaich na hÉireann* after the Volunteers; the Provisional Government sought to portray the NA as the true inheritors of the IRA and it provided the basis for the modern Irish Army.

It was perhaps inevitable that the NA organization was heavily influenced by that of the British Army but retained the ranks used by the Volunteers/IRA until January 1923. The revised rank system bore closer resemblance to those used by other armies although the IRA title commandant was retained in preference to the more commonly used rank of major.

Unlike the Republicans the Saorstát was able to draw on British resources to equip its forces. The British Government was willing to supply arms and equipment in large quantities and was even prepared to loan troops if asked. When NA troops shelled the Four Courts they did so using borrowed British guns firing borrowed ammunition. Even the NA's uniforms were manufactured in Britain.

Although the NA pre-dated the civil war it was during the conflict that its expansion was most rapid. In July 1922 the Dáil authorized an establishment of 35,000 men but by May 1923 it had grown to 53,000. This in itself created major problems as the NA lacked the expertise necessary to train and fight with a force of that size. Approximately 20 per cent of its officers and 50 per cent of its soldiers had served in the British Army and men like Henry Kelly VC, MC and Bar, Martin Doyle VC, MM, W.R.E. Murphy DSO and Bar, MC, and Emmet Dalton MC brought considerable combat experience to it.

Others were not so useful and one of the first courts martial was of an ex-British NCO, Sergeant-Major Dixon, who was charged with mutiny and insubordination.

Ill discipline plagued the NA as half-trained troops were thrown into fighting that most taxing of operations – a counter-insurgency campaign. Although there was considerable combat experience in the NA, there was very little in the way of administrative, logistical and training experience to accompany it. Some units were of course better than others and the Dublin Guards became the shock troops of the Saorstát.

The Dublin Guards were an eclectic mix of IRA veterans loyal to Collins and ex-Royal Dublin Fusiliers who earned a fearsome reputation in Co. Kerry for brutality that persists to this day. Their commander, Brigadier Paddy Daly, one-time OC (officer commanding) of Collins' special unit 'the Squad', once commented that 'nobody had asked me to take kid gloves to Kerry so I didn't'.

The NA proved both willing and able to execute prisoners and carry out reprisals. In all they executed 77 men under the Public Safety Act whilst many others were shot out of hand. The worse atrocity took place at Ballyseedy, Co. Kerry, in March 1923 when nine Republicans were tied to a mine and blown up.

As the NA grew the Provisional Government attempted to create a command structure to manage it. Only General W.R.E. Murphy had higher command experience, having been a British Army brigadier-general during World War I. Major-General Dalton had been a major in the British Army whilst Lieutenant-General J.J. O'Connell and Major-General John Prout had both fought in the US Army during World War I.

Originally GHQ created three Military Districts (Eastern, Western and Southern) but in July 1922 these expanded to eight regional commands that were reorganized again in January 1923 into nine. Collins was

Some of the last British soldiers marching down the North Wall, Dublin, to embark for England, marking the end of the British military presence in Southern Ireland. (Corbis)

NA Commander in Chief but was replaced by Chief of Staff Mulcahy after his death in August 1922. Mulcahy was also the Saorstát Minister of Defence and this dual role as politician and soldier created a degree of unease amongst several TDs, including Home Affairs Minister Kevin O'Higgins.

The infantry dominated the NA and by January 1923 it had over 60 battalions. British-supplied armoured cars, armoured personnel carriers, artillery and aeroplanes and had also brought about the creation of the cavalry, artillery and air corps. An air corps Bristol Fighter flown by an RAF veteran provided close air support during the NA attack on Blessington, Co. Dublin in July 1922 and by mid-1923 the NA had 27 machines supporting ground operations from bases at Baldonnel, Co. Dublin and Fermoy, Co. Cork.

After the civil war demobilization was another headache for the Irish Government and the problems of reducing the size of the NA and how to deal with ex-servicemen would dog Irish politics well into the 1930s.

Britain ensured that the Free State was supplied with modern weapons, such as this Rolls-Royce armoured car. (Corbis)

Thanks to the efforts of the IRA during the Anglo-Irish War and the withdrawal of the Royal Irish Constabulary (RIC) after the Treaty, law and order had broken down in much of Ireland. The situation was further aggravated by the competing ambitions of the Republicans and Saorstát to be recognized as the legitimate government. As a result the Saorstát established the Civic Guards in February 1922 as its new constabulary.

From the start the influence of the RIC on the new force was apparent. Initially armed, several of its senior officers had served in the RIC, as had its first recruit, P.J. Kerrigan, who was also an ex-Irish Guardsman. The Civic Guards played little part in the civil war, being overshadowed by the NA. In September 1922 it ceased to be an armed force and was renamed *An Garda Síochána* in August 1923, which remains the title of the Irish Police.

Free State troops fight through a building during the street battle for Dublin in July 1922. (Image courtesy of the National Library of Ireland)

The British

Unlike the Home Rule and Government of Ireland Acts, the Treaty made provision for an Irish Defence Force based on the IRA and there was even talk of transferring the existing Irish regiments into it. Consequently, immediately after the Treaty was signed the British began to hand over their barracks and withdraw their troops from Southern Ireland. The only exception was a force of some 5,000 men under the command of General Macready based in Dublin that finally left in December 1922.

When the civil war broke out only the British had conducted any contingency planning and it was the threat of armed intervention during the Four Courts occupation by IRA Irregulars that helped galvanize the Saorstát into action. When Collins and de

Valera announced their electoral pact in the summer of 1922 the British had suspended all troop withdrawals with an explicit threat of renewed conflict if the Provisional Government failed to honour the Treaty.

Throughout the civil war there was close liaison between NA and British forces and British intelligence officers continued to conduct covert operations in Southern Ireland. In Northern Ireland the IRA was seen very much as a police matter and the newly formed Royal Ulster Constabulary (RUC) and Ulster Special Constabulary (USC, also known as the 'B' Specials) bore the brunt of internal security operations.

The RUC was effectively a repackaged RIC right down to its green uniforms and insignia whilst the Specials were predominantly a part-time force raised mainly from the Ulster Protestant community. The fact that many Specials were also members of the UVF caused controversy at the time and this image blighted the 'B' Specials until they were disbanded in 1970.

The Anglo-Irish peace and the Republicans

Although the ceasefire of July 1921 effectively brought to an end the phase of the hostilities known as the Anglo-Irish War, few knew it at the time. Both the British and the IRA used it as a breathing space to re-arm, gather intelligence and limber up for the next round.

During the London peace negotiations in the autumn and winter of 1921 the British Prime Minister, Lloyd George, continually pressured the Irish negotiators with threats of renewed violence on a scale hitherto unseen. Lloyd George wanted a swift resolution to the peace talks and did not

The Irish plenipotentiaries who negotiated with the British in the winter of 1921. From left to right: Arthur Griffith, Edmund J Duggan, Erskine Childers, Michael Collins, Gavan Duffy, Robert Barton and John Chartres. © Hulton-Getty Library

really seem to care how Ireland was governed as long as it retained the monarchy and remained within the Empire, supporting British strategic interests in the Atlantic.

Collins and Griffith had to gamble that Lloyd George was bluffing about renewing hostilities. At best the IRA had achieved a military stalemate and Collins admitted that he 'recognized our inability to beat the British out of Ireland'. If the British were bluffing then so were the Irish.

Lloyd George gave Collins no opportunity to refer the document back to Dublin for approval. The choice was simple: was it to be war or peace? Lloyd George, ever the consummate politician, had called Collins' bluff and Collins had no choice but to fold. Consequently, outclassed and outmanoeuvred, the Irish delegates signed

the Anglo-Irish Treaty at 2.10am on
6 December 1921. Prophetically Collins
even quipped that he was signing his own
death warrant.

In essence the Treaty confirmed the
partition of Ireland enshrined in the 1920
Government of Ireland Act and its provisions
applied almost exclusively to the 26 counties
of what is now the Irish Republic. As far as
Northern Unionists were concerned the 1920
Act was the final settlement to the issue of
Home Rule and, much to de Valera's chagrin,
they refused to take part in the negotiations
despite Lloyd George's efforts.

The Treaty also ensured that the new Irish
Free State or Saorstát Éireann retained the
king as head of state. Erskine Childers, the
Anglo-Irish secretary to the Irish negotiators
and ardent Republican, was horrified that
'Irish Ministers would be the King's Ministers'
and worse still for Republicans the Saorstát
would be a Dominion within the British
Empire and Commonwealth. Famously
Collins said that it might not be 'the ultimate
freedom that all nations aspire and develop,
but the freedom to achieve freedom'.

Republicans objected to the oath
of allegiance contained in the Treaty.
Ironically both Collins and de Valera had

been involved in drafting the oath and as
oaths of allegiance go it was fairly
innocuous. It required 'allegiance to the
constitution of the Irish Free State' and to
be 'faithful to HM King George V' whereas
Britons swore 'by Almighty God that I will
be faithful and bear true allegiance to HM
King George V' alone. Loyalty was primarily
to the constitution of the Saorstát and
Collins had even gained the approval
of the IRB before accepting it.

Ultimately the Treaty was a compromise
and Collins and its supporters knew it.
De Valera was furious when he heard that
it had been signed without his consent.
Both the Irish historians and commentators
Ryle Dwyer and P.S. O'Hegarty have claimed
that de Valera's objections had much
more to do with wounded pride than
his Republican beliefs. According to Irish
historian Ronan Fanning, his objections
were more about its being someone else's
compromise rather than his own.

The Treaty also left the British in control
of three naval bases within the Free State.

Liam Mellows photographed at the grave of Wolfe Tone
in 1922. One of de Valera's strongest supporters, he
predicted an early war against Britain, believing her
to be the "only enemy" of Ireland. (Corbis)

De Valera's instructions to Irish Treaty negotiation
delegates were quite clear: they were authorized to
negotiate and conclude a treaty without having to refer
to the Dáil.

TO ALL TO WHOM THESE PRESENTS COME, GREETING:

In virtue of the authority vested in me by
DAIL EIREANN, I hereby appoint

Arthur Griffith, T.D., Minister for Foreign Affairs, Chairm

Michael Collins, T.D., Minister for Finance,

Robert C. Barton, T.D., Minister for Economic Affairs,

Edmund J. Duggan, T.D.,

George Gavan Duffy, T.D.

as Envoys Plenipotentiary from the Elected Government of the
REPUBLIC OF IRELAND to negotiate and conclude on behalf of
Ireland with the representatives of his Britannic Majesty,
GEORGE V., a Treaty or Treaties of Settlement, Association
and Accommodation between Ireland and the community of nations
known as the British Commonwealth.

IN WITNESS WHEREOF I hereunto subscribe my name
as President.

Done in the City of Dublin   Eamon De Valera
this 7th day of October in
the year of our Lord 1921
in five identical originals.

The IRA Divided: January 1922

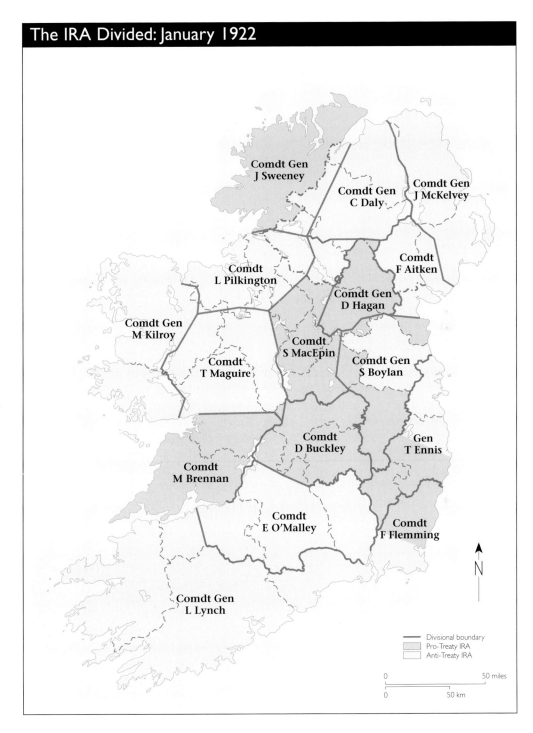

Comdt Gen
J Sweeney

Comdt Gen
C Daly

Comdt Gen
J McKelvey

Comdt
F Aitken

Comdt
L Pilkington

Comdt Gen
D Hagan

Comdt Gen
M Kilroy

Comdt
S MacEpin

Comdt
T Maguire

Comdt Gen
S Boylan

Comdt
D Buckley

Gen
T Ennis

Comdt
M Brennan

Comdt
E O'Malley

Comdt
F Flemming

N

Comdt Gen
L Lynch

— Divisional boundary
Pro-Treaty IRA
Anti-Treaty IRA

0   50 miles

0   50 km

Childers thought that this was 'the most humiliating condition that can be inflicted on any nation claiming to be free'. It also left British troops in Dublin as insurance until the new state had been established.

The Dáil began debating the Treaty on 14 December and finally voted by a narrow margin of 64 to 57 in favour of it. In many respects the Dáil was probably not the best place for the debate as virtually all its

members were dedicated Republicans. That
is no doubt why the debates were so bitter;
personal rivalries soon bubbled to the surface
and many opponents to the Treaty felt that
Cathal Brugha's vitriolic attacks on Collins
cost them key votes. Similar exchanges also
ensued between Childers and Griffith.

De Valera claimed that if he 'wanted
to know what the Irish people wanted
I only had to examine my heart', ably
demonstrating what Charles Townshend
described as a Robespierrist tendency to
tell people what they were thinking rather
than ask them. He also claimed that
regardless of the debate the Dáil had the
authority to dissolve neither itself nor the
Republic, which was what would effectively
happen if the Treaty were accepted.

Opponents saw it as a betrayal of
everything they had fought for since 1916
and Liam Mellows was adamant that the
delegates 'had no power to sign away the
rights of Ireland and the Irish Republic'.
In the minds of many, Irish independence
and the Irish Republic had become one and
the same thing and they could not conceive
of one without the other.

The problem faced by Republicans
was that not all their countrymen felt as
passionately about 'the Republic' as they did.
Sinn Féin's landslide victory in the 1918
General Election had been as much about

Comdt Paddy Daly, the man who "…didn't take the kid
gloves to Co Kerry…" inspects the Dublin Guards.
(Image courtesy of the National Library of Ireland)

protests against the introduction of
conscription and the lack of a credible
Nationalist alternative after the collapse
of the IPP as it was an endorsement of
the Irish revolution.

It is important to remember that Sinn Féin
in 1918 was not the same unitary party as its
modern equivalent but an umbrella
organization for a whole host of constitutional
Nationalist as well as 'physical force'
Republicans. Its main unifying factor had been
the process of undoing the 1801 Act of Union,
so, whilst these differences had been relatively
contained during the Anglo-Irish War, within
days of the Treaty's signature the threads that
bound it together began to unravel.

By Christmas 1921 24 Southern county
councils had passed resolutions in support
of the Treaty. Nevertheless, between the Dáil
vote and the General Election in June 1922
opponents of the Treaty attempted to prevent
any sort of plebiscite on the issue being held.
Rory O'Connor even implied that the IRA
should stage a coup d'etat and impose its own
authority if the politicians failed to defend the
Republic. None of this did anything to
reassure the British Government of the
stability of the fledgling Saorstát.

Nor did it reassure the Unionists in Northern Ireland. Many Northern Protestants saw Northern Catholics as the enemy within and according to Peter Hart sectarian violence forced at least 8,000 people from their homes in Belfast alone. Meanwhile the IRA's campaign continued in what some Republicans called the 'occupied six counties' of Ulster. There was sectarian violence in the South but not to the same degree as in the North.

In response to the anti-Catholic pogroms taking place in the North Sinn Féin and the IRA had instigated a boycott of Northern businesses known as the 'Belfast Boycott'. Sir Edward Carson had once commented that 'Ulster might be wooed by sympathetic understanding – she can never be coerced.' The boycott and attacks on Southern Protestants did nothing to reassure Northern Loyalists and simply reinforced their fears of becoming subsumed in a Catholic Irish state.

Left to right: Generals Tom Ennis, Èoin O'Duffy and Emmet Dalton take the salute as National Army troops take control of Portobello Barracks, Dublin in February 1922. © Hulton-Getty Library

In January and March 1922 the Unionist leader, Sir James Craig, and Collins made what became known as the 'Craig–Collins Agreements', which sought to end the boycott in the South and sectarian violence in the North. Both pacts failed to achieve their goals and Unionist obfuscation of the boundary commission established under the Treaty ensured that many issues surrounding the border were unresolved until the 1998 Good Friday Agreement.

Northern Unionists had not wanted devolution in 1914 or 1920 but if Britain was imposing a local parliament on them then Loyalists were determined that it would make reunification with the South impossible. Some even saw Dominion status for 'Ulster' as the answer and in December 1922, at the height of the Southern civil war, Northern Ireland formally voted to reject membership of the Saorstát, as the Anglo-Irish Treaty offered them the opportunity to do.

For the IRA the truce was a mixed blessing. Both Collins and Mulcahy knew how weak the IRA's military capability really was although many of its activists had convinced themselves that they had achieved victory not

stalemate. IRA ranks swelled with what veteran guerrillas sneeringly called 'truciliers' who did not share their dedication to the Republic they had fought and suffered for. On the whole this hardcore of the IRA opposed the Treaty and some, like Tom Barry, saw renewal of hostilities as the only way to save Republican unity.

Shortly before de Valera resigned as President of the Dáil in January 1922, to be replaced by Arthur Griffith, GHQ had reassured him that the IRA would support the Government; but in reality it was as divided as Sinn Féin. Collins and Mulcahy supported the Treaty along with Eoin O'Duffy (Deputy Chief of Staff), J.J. O'Connell (Assistant Chief of Staff), Diarmuid O'Hegarty (Director of Organization), Emmet Dalton (Director

A motorized anti-Treaty IRA group patrols Sligo Town to prevent a pro-Treaty rally on Sunday 16 April 1922. During the war both sides made extensive use of motor vehicles to transport troops. (Image courtesy of Donal MacCarron)

of Training) and Piaras Béalsaí (Director of Publicity).

Fortunately for the Saorstát those staff officers who declared against the Treaty – Rory O'Connor (Director of Engineering), Liam Mellows (Director of Purchases), Seán Russell (Director of Munitions) and Seamus O'Donovan (Director of Chemicals) – did not head the operations and training branches of the IRA. This lack of expertise would become apparent as the civil war progressed.

Seán MacEntee, a Belfast-born anti-Treaty Republican politician, warned the Dáil that, 'We are now upon the brink of civil war in Ireland. Let there be no mistake about that.' Even opponents of the Treaty like Seán Hegarty came to believe that civil war simply gave the British an excuse for 'coming back in'. Michael Hayes TD was convinced that Collins' and Mulcahy's influence in the IRA was crucial and many men went pro-Treaty simply because it was 'good enough for Mick'.

8 May 1922: pro- and anti-Treaty IRA officers meet at the Mansion House, Dublin to attempt to avert civil war. Left to right: General Seán MacÈoin, Sean Moylan, General Èoin O'Duffy, Liam Lynch, Gearóid O'Sullivan and Liam Mellows. © George Morrison

Now pro- and anti-Treaty IRA faced each other in an uneasy peace. The Provisional Government's solution to the rift in the IRA was to create a new National Army. On 16 January 1922 it made its first public appearance, when men of what would become the Dublin Guards paraded in Dublin Castle and Collins received the keys from the Lord Lieutenant, formally ending 800 years of 'British' rule.

Meanwhile the British were handing over their bases across Southern Ireland to IRA units regardless of their sympathies. Consequently the Dublin-based Provisional Government did not control large areas of Ireland 'beyond the Pale' and low-level IRA violence continued in some areas, with over 52 RIC members being killed in the first half of 1922. Of more concern was the fact that some IRA units began publicly to reject the authority of GHQ and Griffith's Provisional Government in Dublin.

The split in the IRA was exacerbated when in March and April 1922 a series of anti-Treaty Army Conventions voted to establish a new Executive and Army Council headed by Liam Lynch as Chief of Staff. Beyond a desire to launch an IRA offensive against the North (which would in fact be launched in May), it seemed there were no unifying factors left.

On 13 April 1922, 180 men from the 1st and 2nd Battalions, Dublin No. 1 Brigade IRA under Commandant Patrick O'Brien occupied the Four Courts in Central Dublin accompanied by most of the members of the Republican Executive. The British saw the occupation as a breach of the Treaty and began planning to remove O'Brien's men even if such action ran the risk of reuniting the IRA.

Table 1. June 1922 Irish General Election Results					
Party	Sinn Féin	Labour Party	Farmers' Party	Independents	Total
Pro-Treaty	58	17	7	10	92
Anti-Treaty	36				36
Total Number of Seats in the 3rd Dáil/Parliament of Southern Ireland					128

Field Marshal Sir Henry Wilson, ex-Chief of the Imperial General Staff and Ulster Unionist MP. It was his assassination in June 1922 that forced the Provisional Government to take action against the IRA in the Four Courts. © Hulton-Getty Library

The following month, in a vain attempt to paper over the cracks in the Republican movement and maintain unity, Collins and de Valera made a pact in the run-up to the 1922 General Election. They agreed that a panel of pro- and anti-Treaty Sinn Féin candidates would stand with the aim of creating a coalition government after the election. The British declared that the pact was a breach of the Treaty and demanded that the Irish should stop trying to avoid implementing it.

In the end Collins repudiated the pact two days before the 16 June election and the Provisional Government published its constitution on polling day. The result was an overwhelming vote in favour of the Treaty and by implication the new Saorstát constitution. Of the 26 counties 78 per cent voted to accept a flawed peace rather than see a continuation of the Troubles, with only 22 per cent of the vote going to anti-Treaty candidates. The majority of the Irish Diaspora (the Irish communities living outside Ireland) within the British Empire and more crucially the USA were also happy to accept the Treaty as an end to the war. The loss of Irish-America was a critical blow to the Republican movement's ability to overturn the Treaty by force.

In March de Valera had warned that if the electorate ratified the Treaty then the IRA would 'have to wade through Irish blood' to achieve freedom. The election results therefore reinforced the pro-Treaty position.

The situation was made worse by the assassination of Field Marshal Sir Henry Wilson MP by the London IRA on 22 June. Although there is no evidence linking Collins to the shooting it was widely believed by many IRA that he, not the Executive, had ordered the killing. The truth is that we will probably never know who ordered the attack as his killers, who had anti-Treaty sympathies, insisted at their trial that they had acted on their own initiative.

The British chose to blame the Executive for killing Wilson because as a Unionist MP and military advisor to the Northern Government many Republicans blamed him for the sectarian violence in Belfast. Nothing could have been further from the truth, however, for despite being an Irish Protestant Wilson was very critical of the Ulster Special Constabulary (USC) and felt that sectarian violence was counter-productive to the Unionist cause.

His death placed Griffith's Provisional Government under increased pressure to act if British intervention was to be avoided and it made the decision to clear the Four Courts. NA troops under Brigadier Paddy Daly cordoned off the courts, capturing Leo Henderson on 27 June in Dublin. This provoked the Executive to order the kidnapping of J.J. 'Ginger' O'Connell as a reprisal.

The kidnapping backfired, as the Executive underestimated O'Connell's popularity with NA troops. Mulcahy had, however, already decided on 26 June to attack the courts and O'Connell's kidnapping simply provided a pretext. At 4am on 28 June 1922 the occupants of the courts were given an ultimatum to surrender. Thirty minutes later the civil war began.

Conflict in Dublin and the provinces

The period formally remembered as the Irish Civil War began at 4.30am on 28 June 1922, when Easter Rising veteran and now NA officer Captain Johnny Doyle, after one misfire and a hefty kick to the breach of his 18lb gun, fired a shell at the Four Courts. However, tensions had been mounting for several months. This shot was not the first to be exchanged between rival members of the IRA since the signing of the Treaty and an uneasy standoff had developed in Limerick in March after inconclusive skirmishes.

Despite low-level violence, many believed that war could be avoided, and according to anti-Treaty IRA Army Council Member Florrie O'Donoghue 'no plans existed on either side for conducting it'. Mulcahy had hoped that by creating an army loyal to the Saorstát he could draw the teeth of the IRA whilst Republicans believed that as long as the 'Ulster Question' remained unresolved their former comrades could be won around, especially if the British could be provoked into action.

Only the British seemed to believe that conflict was possible and planned accordingly. In the first six months of 1922 they had supplied over 3,504 grenades, 11,900 rifles, 4,200 revolvers and 79 machine guns to the NA, with sufficient ammunition to service them, and maintained 5,000 troops in Dublin just in case. Unbeknown to the British, Collins redirected many of these weapons to ensure that the IRA in Northern Ireland was sufficiently equipped to prosecute operations against the Stormont regime.

Despite upping the ante by occupying the Four Courts and several other locations in Dublin, Republican forces failed to seize the initiative, squandering the only opportunity they had to win a war against the Saorstát and their British backers. To win they needed a quick victory, one that would rapidly neutralize the NA and its long-term

material advantage. In short, nothing less than a *coup de main* against their former comrades would suffice.

Instead they chose to virtually replicate the excessively military gesture of Easter 1916 and seize key points in Dublin then simply sit back and await the consequences. With most of the rebel Executive's members holed up in the Four Courts they were unable to direct operations in Munster or any other Republican stronghold. It was a failing that characterized the strategic direction of their operations throughout the war.

In essence the military conduct of the Irish Civil War can be divided into three distinct phases. The first, from 28 June to 5 July 1922, was almost a rerun of Easter week 1916. The second, from 5 July until 19 August 1922, was dominated by Saorstát assaults on Republican strongholds in the west and south of Ireland, whilst the third and final phase, which ended in May 1923, saw the IRA revert to the guerrilla tactics used against the British.

Unlike the IRA of 1919–21 the civil war IRA lacked popular support, which eventually led its Chief of Staff, Frank Aiken, to issue an order on 24 May 1923 for his men to dump arms and go home. The war was effectively over, although, much as with the Truce of 1921, few realized it at the time. Although the pro-Treaty faction had won, it was a far from decisive victory and, to misappropriate the words of T.S. Eliot's poem *The Hollow Men*, the conflict had ended 'Not with a bang but a whimper'.

Dublin, 28 June–5 July 1922

The Republicans' lack of strategic thought was exemplified by the presence of 12 of the Executive's 16 members in the Four Courts, including Chief of Staff Joe McKelvey, Rory O'Connor and Liam Mellows abrogating their command responsibilities and acting as common soldiers. Contained within a small area of Dublin they were unable to direct operations elsewhere.

Commandant O'Brien worked out plans for the defence of the Four Courts with Ernie O'Malley (OC 2nd Southern Division) and Oscar Traynor (OC Dublin No. 1 Brigade). Since April they had been fortifying the complex with sandbags, trenches and mines but O'Malley knew that he needed at least another 70 men to defend it properly.

Equipped with a number of automatic weapons as well as rifles and a Rolls Royce armoured car, 'the Mutineer', the Republicans sat back and waited. The NA negated much of 'the Mutineer's' value by blocking the exits to the Four Courts with two disabled Lancia armoured cars. Outgunned, O'Brien planned to hold the

A National Army field gun shells the 'Block' from the junction of Henry Street and O'Connell Street in Dublin, July 1922. (Corbis)

Four Courts and some of its neighbouring buildings whilst sympathizers from outside Dublin surrounded the encircling Provisional Government troops.

The flaw in the plan was that in order to maintain the moral high ground no coherent orders for a Republican offensive on Dublin were issued. The Executive wanted the Provisional Government's forces to fire the first shot and thus bear the blame for starting the war. In the end all this course of action achieved was to give the NA a free hand to clear Republican forces out of the capital.

To counter the Republican threat in Dublin the Provisional Government had roughly 4,000 troops, drawn from Daly's Dublin Guards and General Tom Ennis' 2nd Eastern Division. Their cordon around the Four Courts took in the Four Courts Hotel, Chancery Place, Bridewell Prison, Jameson's Distillery and St Michan's Church. In addition two field guns borrowed from the British were deployed south of the Liffey on Winetavern Street under the command of Major-General Dalton.

The Fighting in Dublin, 28 June–5 July 1922

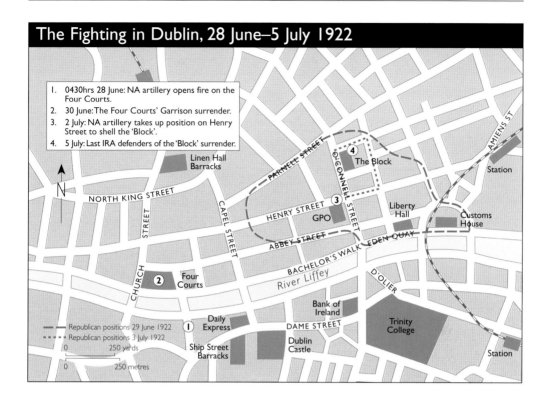

1. 0430hrs 28 June: NA artillery opens fire on the Four Courts.
2. 30 June: The Four Courts' Garrison surrender.
3. 2 July: NA artillery takes up position on Henry Street to shell the 'Block'.
4. 5 July: Last IRA defenders of the 'Block' surrender.

Republican positions 29 June 1922
Republican positions 3 July 1922

0   250 yards
0   250 metres

Dalton's experience in World War I had taught him that 'the use of these guns would have a very demoralizing effect upon a garrison unused to artillery fire'. His gunners lacked training and the meagre supply of shrapnel shells from the British made him conclude erroneously that 'as a destructive agent against the Four Courts building [the guns] would be quite insignificant'. He also saw the guns as a morale booster for his own men and dreaded running out of ammunition.

As the fighting that had started with Doyle's first shot on 28 June progressed, every effort was made to locate ex-British gunners to service the guns and at one point Dalton, an ex-infantryman, was reduced to laying and firing one of the guns himself. Admittedly this was not too difficult a task as they were being fired over open sights across the Liffey into the Four Courts.

Unfortunately this meant that his gunners were well within rifle range of the enemy and on occasion shells punched their way through the building and landed in the grounds of the British HQ just outside of Phoenix Park. During the fighting Dalton met regularly with the British commander, General Macready, and petitioned him for additional guns and ammunition.

Alfred Cope, the British Assistant Under-Secretary in Dublin, believed that if the NA failed to clear the Courts then the Saorstát would be finished. The British feared that the longer the indecisive assault on the Republicans continued, just as in 1916, the more likelihood that the public would begin to sympathize with them. Churchill knew that direct British military intervention would be fatal for the Provisional Government and issued instructions to 'tell Collins to ask for any assistance he requires and report to me any difficulty that has been raised by the military'.

From the start the NA attack on the Four Courts did not go well and according to Cope it was '... not a battle. Rory is in the Four Courts. Free Staters are in the houses opposite each firing at the other hundreds of rounds with probably remarkably few hits. A few hundred yards away the people carry on their ordinary business.'

Although the southern wing of the Four Courts had sustained damage it was insufficient to break the defenders, causing the British to offer heavy artillery and close air support sporting Irish colours to finish the job. Machine gun fire from 'the Mutineer' was a constant nuisance to Dalton's gunners and they were forced to take cover behind a couple of parked Lancia armoured cars. In the end a supply of British shells from Carrickfergus improved the effectiveness of Dalton's guns.

The British had initially supplied 20 shrapnel shells per gun and Dalton was worried that he would run out of ammunition. Macready duly handed over

two more guns and 50 extra shrapnel shells which he insisted were 'all we had left, simply to make noise through the night', as Dalton was afraid that his men would lose heart and drift off if the guns fell silent.

Elsewhere in Dublin there were attempts to mobilize IRA units sympathetic to the Executive's cause. Traynor's Dublin No. 1

Brigade mobilized on the evening of 27 June but disbanded later that night. This was not really such a surprise when the best officers in the brigade were either pro-Treaty or already holed up in the Four Courts. When fighting did break out IRA veteran Emmet Humphreys recalled that 'There seemed no question of co-ordinating our operations with adjoining companies or with the battalion as a whole.'

Not all the Executive's members were bottled up with O'Connor, however. Tom Barry was in custody, having been arrested whilst he was trying to join him in the Four Courts disguised as a woman. Lynch had set up his headquarters in the Clarence Hotel and on 28 June made his way to Kingsbridge Station, where he was arrested by NA troops but released on Mulcahy's orders. He headed west and set up a Republican HQ in Limerick.

Despite envisaging a guerrilla campaign, Traynor had been convinced by his supporters in Tipperary and Belfast that holding part of central Dublin was the best course of action. On 29 June, whilst Lynch was establishing his HQ in Limerick, Traynor occupied the Gresham, Crown, Granville, and Hammam hotels on the east side of O'Connell Street, which became known as 'the Block'.

Republican elements of Dublin No. 1 Brigade also occupied Barry's Hotel in north Dublin and several buildings on the South Circular Road, York Street, the Kildare Street Club and Dolphin's Barn. There was no military logic to the positions and, as Humphreys pointed out, little mutual support. It was at this point that de Valera, Brugha, Stack and Seán T. O'Kelly came out in favour of the Executive and joined those occupying O'Connell Street.

De Valera rejoined his old unit, 3rd Battalion, as an ordinary volunteer and issued a statement that '... at the bidding of

Dublin, 30 June 1922: Free State artillery on the junction of Winetavern Street and Merchant's Quay looking towards the Four Courts. The gunners used disabled armoured lorries to protect them from small-arms fire from across the river. The disabled Lancia APC used by Dalton to block the entrance to the Four Courts can be seen in the distance. © Hulton-Getty Library

the English Irishmen today are shooting down, on the streets of our capital, brother Irishmen. In Rory O'Connor and his comrades lives the unbought indomitable soul of Ireland.' The *Irish Times* reported that de Valera 'has associated himself openly with the men firing on Irish homes'.

Privately de Valera, the sole surviving leader of the 1916 Rising, had grave concerns about the fighting and was in favour of a peace initiative proposed by the Lord Mayor of Dublin and the Labour Party. Brugha and Stack were not so keen, whilst de Valera's refusal to take a leading role ensured that his views were marginalized. Throughout the civil war the Republican political and military leaderships failed to coordinate their efforts, leading ultimately to disaster.

The piecemeal nature of the Republican defence allowed the NA to concentrate its efforts against the Four Courts almost unhindered by the IRA stationed elsewhere in the city even though, according to General MacMahon, the NA troops outside the Four Courts were exhausted. Within the complex the situation was even worse.

O'Malley, who was inside the Four Courts, later wrote that 'it seemed a haphazard pattern of war. A garrison without proper food, surrounded on all sides, bad communications between their inside posts, faulty defences, girls bringing ammunition from attackers, relieving forces on our side concentrated on the wrong side of the widest street in the capital.' Cut off and without support, their position was increasingly hopeless.

By 30 June the NA troops had recovered from their initial failure to storm the Four Courts and, bayonets fixed, forced their way into the complex. In the end it was a short sharp fight that culminated in what Tim Pat Coogan described as one of the greatest acts of vandalism ever perpetrated in Dublin, when Republicans detonated two pre-planted mines under the Public Records Office – although Hopkinson blames NA shelling for detonating the mines.

An anti-Treaty IRA patrol on Grafton Street during the fighting in Dublin. Their appearance is typical of IRA Irregulars during the civil war. © Hulton-Getty Library

A column of smoke rose over 200ft in the air as the ensuing fire consumed centuries-old documents. For hours fragments of ancient documents floated over Dublin and the event led Churchill to write to Collins after the fighting saying that, 'The archives of the Four Courts may be scattered but the title-deeds of Ireland are safe.'

Even faced with a hopeless situation Mellows and O'Connor wanted to fight on in the spirit of Patrick Pearse's 1916 call for a blood sacrifice. Heroic though it may have been, the defence of the Four Courts had

been poorly planned and organized from the start. Seán Smith later claimed that even though they could plainly see Saorstát soldiers taking up positions around their own in the Four Courts they did nothing, as 'we had no orders to fire on them'.

According to Ben Doyle, another Republican survivor, 'the whole thing was taken in a half-hearted slipshod manner'. The tidal ebb and flow of the Liffey made escape through the sewers impossible and in the end Traynor overruled the Executive's insistence upon a last stand and ordered his men in the

Four Courts to surrender. Only O'Brien seemed to realize that it was vital to get the members of the Executive out of the Four Courts. O'Malley and Seán Lemass managed to get out through Jameson's Distillery but O'Connor and Mellows surrendered.

With the battle for the Four Courts over, the Provisional Government shifted its main effort onto isolating O'Connell Street. Republican efforts in the rest of the city proved to be of little value and by 3 July most of their positions south of the Liffey had fallen. Thus, free from the danger of

being attacked in the rear the Saorstát's forces massed around the Republican positions in 'the Block' to administer the *coup de grace*.

Fighting in a built-up area is one of the most complicated, manpower-intensive and bloody operations that any soldier can be called upon to perform and requires levels of discipline, determination and training that neither the NA or Republican forces

possessed. Instead of fighting from house to house and room to room with grenade, bayonet and rifle butt both sides settled down to sniping and inconclusive firefights.

Time, however, was on the side of the Provisional Government and as Republican manpower and ammunition dwindled those of the NA increased. Much as the British had done in 1916 the NA relied upon artillery to shell the Republicans into submission. For the

second time in six years the guns of its own government's army flattened central Dublin.

One by one the Republicans evacuated their positions as concentrated artillery and machine gun fire rendered them untenable. The IRA were accused of using Red Cross vehicles as fire positions and Daly, no shrinking violet himself, claimed they were the 'dirtiest lot of fighters he ever saw'. The situation was made worse when NA

Commandant O'Connor was fired upon whilst attempting to accept the surrender of the forces in the Hammam Hotel on 5 July. In many ways it was a sign of things to come.

Even before the end came Republicans trapped in O'Connell Street knew it was only a matter of time before they would have to accept defeat. Several Republican leaders, including de Valera, were smuggled out across the river to Mount Street, which is a fair indication of how lax the cordon was and how poor the discipline of the NA soldiery. Those who could do so began to leave Dublin and seek shelter in the Republican heartlands to the south-west.

By 5 July one side of O'Connell Street was in flames from St. Mary's Pro-Cathedral to Findlater Place. By late afternoon the only Republican troops left were under the command of Cathal Brugha. Faced with a hopeless situation he ordered his remaining 15 men to surrender and then with suicidal courage ran into the street, gun in hand. The outcome was inevitable and he died of his wounds later that evening in Mater Hospital.

It was estimated that £3m–4m of damage had been done to central Dublin with a butcher's bill of 65 killed and 281 wounded, which compared to the casualties of Easter week 1916 meant that both Dubliners and the combatants had come off lightly. The capture of several key members of the Executive also ensured that the Republican leadership was severely weakened at the start of the civil war.

Lynch was the one major Republican military leader still at large and he swiftly abandoned the Dublin-centric strategy of O'Connor and the others now languishing in Mountjoy Gaol. Having established his HQ in Limerick he reasserted himself as the Chief of Staff of Republican forces and ordered his divisional commanders to return to their formations rather than converge on the capital. From here on in the Republicans' war effort would be quite literally beyond the Pale.

The Four Courts Record Office ablaze shortly before the Republican surrender. (Corbis)

ABOVE Armed men behind a barricade in a Dublin
street during the fighting in Dublin. (Corbis)

BELOW National Army soldiers escort a wounded
IRA prisoner during the fighting in Dublin. © George
Morrison

5 July–19 August 1922

The St John's Ambulance personnel give first aid to a wounded soldier on O'Connell Street, July 1922.
© Hulton-Getty Library

Again there are parallels between IRA activity outside Dublin in the events of Easter 1916 and June 1922. As in 1916 the forces were divided and confused orders were issued and countermanded. In response to an appeal from Traynor, Mick Sheehan and over 100 men from South Tipperary occupied Blessington, Co. Dublin on 1 July 1922 with the intent of marching on the capital 15 miles away.

Over 200 men from the South Dublin Brigade and Kildare IRA as well as escapees from the fighting in Dublin soon joined them. Traynor had confused the issue by telling Sheehan 'neither to march on Dublin nor defend Blessington if attacked'. By the time he and O'Malley arrived in Blessington on 6 July he was convinced that a counter-attack on Dublin was impossible with the troops at hand and ordered them to revert to guerrilla tactics.

His orders were probably recognition of a degenerating situation and on 8 July a Republican report recommended that the men dump arms. O'Malley took some men with him to occupy towns in Co. Wexford but many others simply went home. The NA response to Sheehan's seizure of Blessington was to dispatch columns from the Curragh, Dublin and the coast to converge on the town.

At Brittas and Ballymore Eustace they captured 73 Irregulars with barely a shot fired and by the time they reached Blessington the fight had gone out of its defenders. Traynor believed that many of his men were 'completely out of their element'. The town was abandoned and Brigadier Andy McDonnell, Gerry Boland and around 100 others were taken prisoner.

The Republican failure to defend Blessington sapped the morale of its fighting men and virtually became the template of their efforts in other towns. Again and again they would abandon strategically vital towns, almost without a shot, when faced with an NA attack. Perhaps the experience of guerrilla warfare against the British made many of the IRA temperamentally unsuited to positional warfare, whilst a complete lack of strategic guidance from the Executive could not have helped.

For the NA, Blessington also provided a template for what was to come. Each of the columns dispatched to retake the town was supplied with artillery, armoured cars and automatic weapons. The nascent Irish Air Corps even flew sorties in support of the offensive and although the British supplied the NA with only nine field guns, artillery support featured in almost every major attack.

In fact the Republicans' lack of artillery vexed Lynch, who exhausted a disproportionate amount of effort in attempting to source guns and instructors from Germany. He even made contact with an obscure German politician by the name of Adolf Hitler in his pursuit of such weapons. Lynch's fixation with artillery betrayed his failure to grasp the realities of the situation.

Whilst the NA lacked trained gunners they had at least access to British assistance and both Collins and Dalton actively sought to recruit British Army veterans. The Republicans, however, did not enjoy such expertise and when Aiken finally captured a field gun at Dundalk on 14 August he was forced to abandon it because no one knew how to operate it. Even if they had retained it,

Provisional Government troops in Claregalway, 20 July 1922. Their appearance is fairly typical of National Army troops at the start of the war. Supply problems meant that it would be several months before they began to look like a regular army. © George Morrison

it is difficult to imagine what useful purpose it would have served in a guerrilla war.

O'Malley's activities in Co. Wexford lacked strategic vision and proved of little value when he abandoned towns in the face of Government troops sent to confront him under the command of Major-General John Prout. The IRA made a brief stand in Waterford but when Captain Ned O'Brien secured the quays on 20 July, allowing Prout to ferry men and artillery into the town, the Republicans surrendered.

Despite their inability to hold static defences, on 9 July Liam Deasy, the anti-Treaty OC 1st Division IRA, claimed that Republican forces were establishing a defensive line from Waterford to Limerick; however, as Hopkinson points out, this never really existed except on paper. Its dubious value was further undermined when Dan Breen and 400 Republicans lost Carrick-on-Suir to Prout's 600-man column on 3 August, effectively abandoning Co. Tipperary to the Government.

In his analysis of the conventional phase of the civil war ('The Irish Civil War 1922–1923: A Military Study of the Conventional Phase 28 June – 11 August 1922', paper delivered New York, 1998), Paul V. Walsh observed that, with the notable exception of NA Major-General Murphy outside Kilmallock, none of the commanders on either side attempted to replicate the trench warfare that typified World War I. That is perhaps what makes the Republican emphasis on a defensive line so strange, especially as they would have been incapable of holding it even if they had managed to construct it.

The fact that few of the World War I veterans on either side had been professional soldiers may also have contributed to their willingness to embrace new technology and adopt innovative tactics. Consequently extensive use was made of mobile forces to impose authority quickly upon areas which indicated a willingness to look forward rather than back for operational solutions.

That does not mean that the Irish forces were blessed with military visionaries whose ideas augured *Blitzkrieg* with its mobile all-arms battlegroups. The Republican use of armoured vehicles to attack Bruree or the NA amphibious attacks on Munster were products of expediency rather than of coherent doctrine and the lessons identified were rapidly forgotten after the war.

Lack of a coherent Republican strategy beyond trying to re-ignite the Anglo-Irish War and poor leadership ensured that the Provisional Government seized the initiative. Both Collins and Mulcahy knew that the British would only withdraw their troops from Southern Ireland if they believed that the Provisional Government had the situation under control. To that end Collins needed a rapid victory and that dictated the pace of NA operations.

Even before the outbreak of violence in Dublin it was obvious that Limerick would be strategically vital in any future conflict. Lynch established his GHQ there on 29 June and the NA commander in the city, Commandant-General Michael Brennan, OC 1st Western Division, believed that 'Whoever held Limerick held the south and the west'.

IRA Irregulars building barricades in Carrick-on-Suir, 20 July 1922 in anticipation of the arrival of General Prout's forces. © George Morrison

Major engagements, June–August 1922

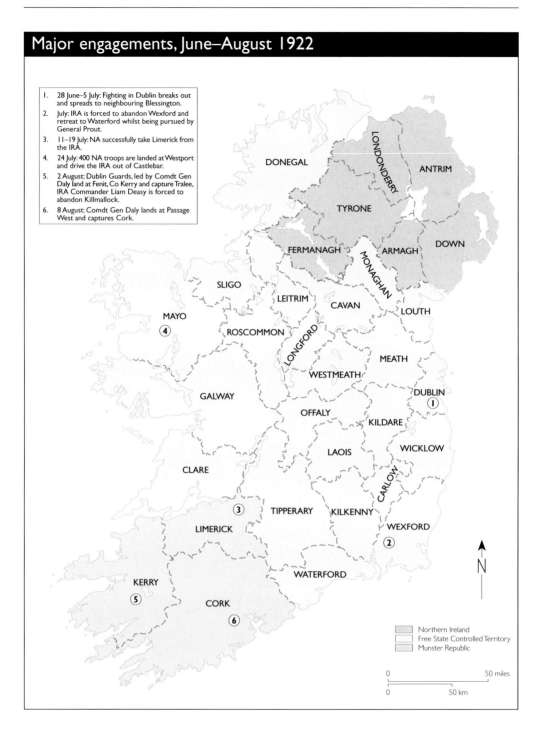

1.   28 June–5 July: Fighting in Dublin breaks out and spreads to neighbouring Blessington.
2.   July: IRA is forced to abandon Wexford and retreat to Waterford whilst being pursued by General Prout.
3.   11–19 July: NA successfully take Limerick from the IRA.
4.   24 July: 400 NA troops are landed at Westport and drive the IRA out of Castlebar.
5.   2 August: Dublin Guards, led by Comdt Gen Daly land at Fenit, Co Kerry and capture Tralee, IRA Commander Liam Deasy is forced to abandon Killmallock.
6.   8 August: Comdt Gen Daly lands at Passage West and captures Cork.

Northern Ireland
Free State Controlled Territory
Munster Republic

0   50 miles
0   50 km

When the local IRA commander Commandant Liam Forde had repudiated GHQ's authority on 18 February Mulcahy had ordered Brennan to occupy the city with his pro-Treaty IRA. Shots were exchanged and it was only the intervention of Lynch and Traynor that averted civil war at that time. The Republicans occupied four barracks and most of the town whilst Saorstát troops, drawn mostly from Commandant-General O'Hannigan's 4th Southern Division, occupied the Customs House, the courthouse, the gaol and Williams Street RIC barracks.

Brennan established his HQ in Cruise's Hotel and secured the strategically important Athlunkard Bridge outside the city, deploying his troops to defend the road that led across it into Limerick. If the situation degenerated he would be able to feed troops into the city via the bridge without hindrance from Republican forces.

As a result of the outbreak of violence in Dublin both Brennan and Lynch made some attempts to defuse the situation in Limerick. On 7 July they negotiated a truce, much to the chagrin of Republicans in Munster who believed that it would give the pro-Treaty forces time to consolidate their positions in the city. On 11 July the truce broke down at 7pm when 150 fresh NA reinforcements arrived in the city and Brennan ordered his men to attack the IRA forces garrisoning the Ordnance Barracks.

Lynch withdrew to Clonmel and ten days later General Èoin O'Duffy with a further 1,500 men, four armoured cars and a field gun arrived to reinforce Brennan. By 19 July the Republicans had been driven out of their positions and Limerick was in Government hands. Casualties had been light with only eight NA soldiers killed and 20 wounded, and 20–30 Republicans killed. More importantly several hundred IRA had been captured and the road to Munster lay open.

The Provisional Government faced similar problems to the British when it came to Republican prisoners and in order to cope with the sheer volume of captured rebels they were forced to open internment camps at the Curragh, Gormanstown and Kilmainham Gaol. By November Limerick Gaol had over 800 inmates in a complex designed to hold only 120.

Like the British before them the Provisional Government decided that internment was counterproductive and on 10 July it released prisoners as part of an amnesty. The Government was resolved to keep captured Republican leaders in prison but it believed that there was little value in keeping the rank and file locked up and was willing to release anyone who signed a pledge not to take up arms against the Saorstát.

Although the British only supplied the National Army with nine field guns, artillery featured in every major operation. Here one of General Murphy's guns is towed over a ruined bridge over the River Maigue during the Kilmallock campaign, August 1922. © George Morrison

Although the NA was making considerable headway in Co. Dublin, Co. Waterford and Co. Limerick, the Republicans did enjoy limited military success. By 4 July they had effectively cleared pro-Treaty troops out of Co. Cork when they took Skibbereen and Listowel. Co. Cork had been the heartland of the Republican struggle against the British and although the local IRA were ambivalent about fighting their former comrades they bitterly opposed the Treaty.

This area of south-west Ireland became known as the 'Munster Republic' and it was this area that the vaunted Waterford–Limerick Line was meant to defend. The fall of Limerick was a blow to the Republican cause but Deasy's successful defence with 2,000 men against O'Duffy's southward thrust towards Kilmallock helped secure the area and stabilize the situation.

The respite was, however, only temporary and on 23 July the NA launched a fresh offensive. Despite taking Bruff, Murphy was quickly dislodged by the Republicans and 76 of his men surrendered. A swift counter-attack retook the town and on 30 July the Dublin Guards stormed Bruree. These were the NA's best troops and after a five-hour firefight with close artillery support they managed to force Deasy's men out.

On 2 August the Republicans attempted to re-take Bruree using three armoured cars but the assault failed. Faced with a degenerating situation Deasy decided to break contact and withdraw towards Kilmallock, pursued by over 3,000 NA troops supported by armoured cars, artillery and aircraft. His situation was made worse when the NA landed troops on the Kerry and Cork coasts.

By the time Murphy entered Kilmallock on 5 August all that remained was what was left of Deasy's rearguard and the only major set-piece battle of the war was over. Waterford had fallen to Prout on 17 July and Colonel Commandant Christopher O'Malley had cleared Co. Mayo of Republicans after landing 400 men, a gun and an armoured car from the SS *Minerva* near Westport on 24 July.

The Republicans had abandoned the town without a fight and O'Malley was able to link up with MacÈoin's forces in Castlebar, Co. Mayo. By the end of the month MacÈoin was able to report to Collins that 'in the Midlands Divisions all posts and positions of military value are in our hands'.

Although the Provisional Government wanted a swift victory it knew that it needed to prepare for a protracted struggle. A call to arms was issued on 6 July that put the National Army on a formal footing with

On board the SS *Arvonia* Maj Gen Dalton (second from left) discusses his plans with his second in command Tom Ennis, August 1922. © George Morrison

Dublin Guards disembark from the SS *Lady Wicklow* at Fenit, Co. Kerry on 2 August 1922. © George Morrison

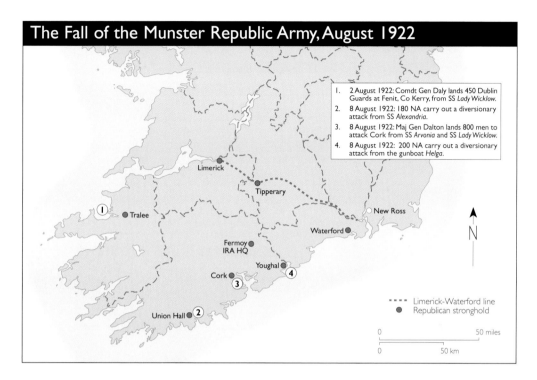

The Fall of the Munster Republic Army, August 1922

1. 2 August 1922: Comdt Gen Daly lands 450 Dublin Guards at Fenit, Co Kerry, from SS Lady Wicklow.
2. 8 August 1922: 180 NA carry out a diversionary attack from SS Alexandria.
3. 8 August 1922: Maj Gen Dalton lands 800 men to attack Cork from SS Arvonia and SS Lady Wicklow.
4. 8 August 1922: 200 NA carry out a diversionary attack from the gunboat Helga.

- - - - Limerick-Waterford line
● Republican stronghold

0   50 miles
0   50 km

an establishment of 20,000 men, finally breaking its links with the 'old' IRA. This would rise to over 58,000 officers and men before the war was over.

In addition Mulcahy abandoned the old IRA divisional boundaries and created five new commands under Dalton (Eastern), MacÈoin (Western), Prout (South-East), O'Duffy (South-West) and O'Connell (Curragh). On 13 July a War Council was established with Collins as Commander in Chief and Mulcahy as Minister of Defence and Chief of Staff.

Cosgrave became Chairman of the Provisional Government and Minister of Finance whilst Griffith remained President of the Dáil, which effectively left two pro-Treaty administrations in charge of the State. In fact the confusing situation of who actually was the government of the Saorstát was not fully resolved until the Dáil and the Southern Irish Parliament finally merged in September 1922. The blurring of jurisdiction suited Collins who until his death was effectively the head of the Irish Government.

The fortunes of the Republicans were further dented on 16 July when the NA

arrested Frank Aiken, OC 4th Northern Division in Dundalk. Despite his objections to the Treaty he had hoped to avert a split in the IRA by staying neutral and focusing attention on the situation in Northern Ireland. When he finally escaped he reluctantly threw in his lot with the Republicans and eventually succeeded Lynch as IRA Chief of Staff.

Traynor was also captured on 27 July whilst Harry Boland was fatally wounded outside the Grand Hotel in Skerries on the 30th. Boland had written earlier in the month to Joe McGarrity of Clan na Gael in the United States asking him, with a degree of irony, if he could 'imagine, me on the run from Mick Collins?' Despite Republican setbacks, Boland had been optimistic about the chances of victory, telling McGarrity that 'I am certain we cannot be defeated even if Collins and his British guns succeed in garrisoning every town in Ireland.'

August saw a renewal of the Provisional Government's offensive in the south-west and a series of victories that were effectively to end the Republicans' conventional military capability. Much as the use of

National Army troops embark on the SS *Arvonia* in Dublin on Monday 7 August 1922. A Peerless armoured car and Lancia APC are being loaded onto the deck and sandbags have been stacked along the waist in anticipation of resistance in Cork. © George Morrison

armoured cars and artillery in Waterford and Limerick were to become hallmarks of NA tactics the amphibious landing in Clew Bay, Co. Mayo which led to the fall of Westport was also to act as a template for later, and decisive, NA operations.

Dalton, NA Director of Operations, believed that a frontal attack on the 'Munster Republic' would be a bloody grinding match and suggested to Collins that a series of amphibious landings in counties Kerry and Cork should secure victory. In modern military terms Dalton was suggesting what would now be called a 'manoeuvrist' approach to the situation, as Republican defences faced inland not seaward. By doing something that was unexpected Dalton was able to overrun the 'Munster Republic' with relatively little bloodshed.

Once more the Dublin Guards acted as the shock troops and 450 of them led by Daly and supported by the ubiquitous armoured car and field gun landed from the SS *Lady Wicklow* at Fenit, Co. Kerry on 2 August. By 6.30pm they had driven Republican elements of No. 1 Kerry Brigade IRA out of Tralee for the loss of nine dead and 35 wounded. The next day Colonel

Commandant Michael Hogan left Co. Clare and crossed the Shannon with 250 men at Kilsrush in fishing boats to reinforce Daly's position. The landing was one of the nails in the coffin of Deasy's defence of Kilmallock.

The real blow fell some six days later when Dalton embarked 800 men, two field guns, three armoured cars and several Lancia armoured personnel carriers on the SS *Arvonia*, SS *Lady Wicklow* and SS *Alexandra*, which were commandeered in Dublin on Monday 7 August for the purpose of invading Co. Cork. The Welsh crew of the *Arvonia* were extremely unhappy with the situation and its captain was convinced that mines would sink his ship before it reached Cork.

Collins had initially asked the British to hand over the naval base at Queenstown as a springboard for an attack on Cork but they had refused. Instead Vice Admiral Somerville, the Royal Navy officer in command of the Southern Irish coastguard, supplied the Provisional Government with details of defensive minefields in the approaches to Cork.

Thus, even without proper charts Dalton's expedition was not as unprepared as the captain of the *Arvonia* believed. Thanks to aerial reconnaissance missions flown by Colonel C.F. Russell of the Irish Air Corps and information from covert intelligence officers in Cork, Dalton also had a fair idea of where the enemy had deployed its forces.

Although the Treaty barred the Saorstát from possessing a navy, as coastal defence remained a British responsibility, the British had handed over several gunboats to the Provisional Government to act as 'revenue cutters'. Amongst them was the *Helga*, the vessel that had shelled Liberty Hall, the HQ of the Citizen Army, and other central Dublin locations in 1916. The *Helga* accompanied Dalton's expedition, probably making it one of the first operations to be carried out by the Irish Navy.

National Army troops from 1st Bn, Dublin Bde land at the Cork Shipbuilding Co. Dock, Passage West, Co. Cork, 8 August 1922. Given the secrecy of the operation the two men in civilian clothes watching them probably belonged to Army intelligence. © George Morrison

According to Coogan the Royal Navy intercepted the expedition and Dalton persuaded them not to compromise him. Considering Somerville's involvement it is more likely that they were dispatched to ensure that Dalton reached the approaches to Cork safely. By 10pm the *Arvonia* was off Roche Point at the mouth to Passage West outside Cork.

It was at this point that *Helga* with 200 men, a field gun and two Lancia armoured personnel carriers sailed for Youghal where they landed without incident. A further 180 men on the *Alexandra* landed at Union Hall, Glandore, in the face of small-arms fire from Republicans in fishing boats. By the time they had managed to unload their armoured car and three armoured personnel carriers, the IRA had melted away and the town was secured.

The troops used at Youghal and Union Hall were for the most part raw recruits whilst Dalton kept hold of 456 men drawn from 1st Battalion, Dublin Brigade on the *Arvonia*. He also hoped that the two diversionary landings would distract the Republicans' attention from his main assault on Cork itself.

His deception was so successful that when the captain of the *Arvonia* requested a pilot to assist in navigating Passage West one was dispatched without any hint of suspicion of the vessel's true intent. When the pilot

National Army soldiers pose with their armoured car. (Image courtesy of the National Library of Ireland)

General John Prout outside his HQ in Carrick-on-Suir, 4 August 1922. Prout had served in the US Army in the Great War. © George Morrison

became reluctant to help, Dalton's threat to shoot him rapidly overcame his misgivings.

Dalton had originally planned to land at Ford's Wharf but the way was barred by a blockship. This meant that the only other unmined deep-water berth available was the Cork Shipbuilding Company's dock at Passage West, which he reached in the early hours of Tuesday 8 August. At 2am Captain Frank Friel and 20 men rowed ashore and discovered that the Republicans had abandoned their posts when they had sighted the *Arvonia* and *Lady Wicklow* entering the harbour.

At dawn Dalton landed 150 men, an armoured car and a gun to establish a defensive cordon about half a mile inland from the berth. Once the area had been secured he off-loaded the rest of his force. IRA Irregular Frank O'Connor observed that, 'Technically, a landing from the sea is supposed to be one of the most difficult military operations, but as we handled the defence it was a walkover.'

Because the Republicans had not anticipated an amphibious attack their troops in the area were, according to IRA Irregular Mick Leahy, the 'poorest type of men'; in the view of Tom Crofts, they had 'been in the line fighting for weeks and they had been brought back there without sleep'. Consequently few were in a position to put up a fight when Dalton landed.

Once the initial shock wore off the Republicans swiftly attempted to block Dalton's advance at Rochestown on the road to Cork where they demolished the bridge leading into the town and fortified several buildings. Exhausted IRA reinforcements were brought in by train from Kilmallock to bolster the defence but as Crofts had pointed out these men were already spent.

By the evening of 8 August the IRA had been shoved out of Rochestown and driven back to Old Court Woods to the west. An attempt to turn their flank on 9 August foundered in the face of massed machine gun and rifle fire from 200 defenders. In the end Captain Friel and Captain Peter Conlon with 12 men secured a Saorstát victory by assaulting Cronin's Cottage on Belmonte Hill and both earned instant promotion to commandant.

Considering the small numbers involved in the battle casualties were relatively high and seven out of 200 IRA and nine out of 456 NA soldiers were killed. According to Walsh there were also a considerable number of wounded to contend with. Amongst the IRA dead was a Scot named Ian MacKenzie Kennedy whom Dalton singled out for his bravery.

Dalton pressed his attack on Thursday 10 August against Douglas on the outskirts of Cork. The battle for Douglas was a confused close-quarter affair involving armoured cars and automatic weapons. Once more Conlon found himself at the point of the spear leading the NA assault and narrowly escaped an IRA ambush when a local woman tipped him off. Supported by eight men he attacked his would-be ambushers, capturing 32 of them.

After three days in contact with the enemy Dalton feared that his men would run out of steam and so intended to pause overnight in Douglas. Much to his surprise his officers pressed for him to push on into the city. True to form the Republicans

Michael Collins at Griffith's funeral in Dublin, 16 August 1922. Suffering from ill health and visibly showing the strain of commanding the Saorstát's forces Collins was killed six days later in an IRA ambush aged just 32 years. (Corbis)

burned their barracks and abandoned Cork. By the evening of 10 August the last Irish city in Republican hands had fallen and the 'Munster Republic' had been overthrown.

Whilst the NA onslaught was underway in Co. Limerick and Co. Cork, Republicans Dinney Lacey and Dan Breen attacked Prout's forces in south Tipperary at Redmondstown on 9 August. Outgunned and subjected to artillery fire, they retreated towards the Nire Valley. On 11 August Lynch abandoned Fermoy, the last Republican stronghold in Co. Cork, to the NA whilst 200 Government troops under the tactical command of Commandant Tom O'Connor landed at Kenmare.

So sudden was the collapse of Republican resistance that the *Irish Times* reported rather optimistically on 16 August that 'the advance is becoming swift but the retreat, or, as I should prefer to call it, the disappearance is swifter'. Predictions of a Republican collapse proved to be premature and the war would drag on for another eight months or so before it fizzled out.

Despite the fact that the NA had driven the IRA out of every major town in the country O'Duffy reported on 22 August that 'the Irregulars in Cork and Kerry are still intact. Our forces have captured towns, but they have not captured Irregulars and arms on anything like a large scale, and, until that is done, the Irregulars will be capable of guerilla warfare ... Our present position leaves us particularly disposed to guerrilla warfare.'

Almost in recognition of their defeat in open warfare the IRA Adjutant General, Con Moloney, issued an order on 19 August for the IRA to abandon conventional operations and form active service units not exceeding 35 men to conduct guerrilla attacks. In addition the IRA authorized its men to commandeer Unionist property for the war effort. The final phase of the war had begun.

The guerrilla war, 19 August 1922–24 May 1923

The guerrilla phase was the longest and in many respects the bitterest stage of the civil war. In all it would last nine months and see an Irish government's frustration manifest itself in a willingness to act ruthlessly.

Although the fall of Cork did much to undermine the Republican cause the Provisional Government suffered a double blow when Griffith died of a brain haemorrhage on 12 August and Collins was killed in an IRA ambush on 22 August at Béal na mBláth, Co. Cork. No one really knows who fired the fatal shot but the most likely candidate is an ex-British soldier, Denis 'Sonny' O'Neill, who was one of the IRA ambushers.

Mulcahy replaced Collins as Commander in Chief, whilst Cosgrave and Kevin O'Higgins provided the civilian leadership of the Provisional Government. All three men envisaged a democratic Ireland with an apolitical army and police serving the Irish people. Consequently all three viewed the Republicans as traitors who sought to destroy their fledgling democracy.

O'Higgins believed that 'soldiers make bad policemen' but had to accept that until

the Civic Guards established themselves the State had no alternative but to use the army to maintain law and order. Ironically, according to Dalton, the Republican guerrillas placed the NA 'in the same position as the British were a little over a year ago'.

Much as the British had before them, the Provisional Government also resorted to harsh legislation to justify their activities against the IRA. The Provisional Government ceased to be 'Provisional' in September 1922 when it oversaw the merger of the Southern Irish Parliament and the Dáil, which became its lower chamber, and approved the Saorstát Constitution. The Senate created by the Government of Ireland Act also continued to act as the upper chamber, providing a forum for Southern Unionists to participate in government. One of its first acts was to pass the Public Safety Act giving emergency powers to the NA. By December the Saorstát had been formally established in British and Irish law and Tim Healy KC was appointed Governor-General.

Unlike the British administration the new Dublin government enjoyed the popular support of the Irish public so when its forces carried out reprisals in response to IRA attacks they tended to be against individuals rather than against property. The emergency powers granted to the NA under the Public Safety Act and, ironically, the still extant Restoration of Order in Ireland Act allowed them to court martial and execute anyone caught illegally carrying weapons.

The first executions took place on 17 November when four Irregulars – Peter Cassidy, James Fisher, John Gaffney and Richard Twohig – were shot in Kilmainham Gaol, Dublin. The policy was controversial from the start and Labour TD Tom Johnson protested but was told by Mulcahy that stern measures were necessary against those 'assassins and wreckers who would destroy the country'. On 24 November Childers was shot under the provisions of the Public Safety Act.

Dalton was uncomfortable with this policy and asked Mulcahy if he was expected to execute the 1,800 Irregulars he had incarcerated in Cork Prison. Although he was

22 August 1922: Michael Collins (in car, far left) leaves Clonakilty, Co Cork with Emmet Dalton. This grainy image was the last picture ever taken of Michael Collins shortly before he was killed in an IRA ambush.

reassured that such an act was not necessary Dalton felt compelled to resign his commission and played no further part in the war. Dalton's gesture did nothing to end the shootings and barely a month went by without a firing squad being convened.

Lynch's response as IRA Chief of Staff was to order the assassination of all TDs who had voted for the Public Safety Act as well as high court judges and hostile newspaper editors. When the IRA assassinated pro-Treaty TD Major-General Seán Hales outside Leinster House on 7 December the Republicans once again totally failed to anticipate the Government's response – the executions of Rory O'Connor, Liam Mellows, Joe McKelvey and Dick Barrett without even the pretence of a trial.

In one respect the reprisals worked as attacks on TDs ceased. Instead the IRA targeted the property of pro-Treaty politicians, burning 37 of their houses in the first two months of 1923, as well as destroying railway stations and lines. The attacks on the railways, especially, did nothing to endear the IRA to the public and they failed to exploit fully the propaganda value of the Government's executions policy. More significantly the rules of engagement were changing.

Not only were IRA prisoners being executed in accordance with the Public Safety Act but, in disturbing echoes of the Anglo-Irish War when death squads on both sides had murdered suspected enemies, NA

troops began to carry out 'unofficial' reprisals and historian Peter Hart notes that Irish officers quickly adopted attitudes towards the IRA similar to those of their former British adversaries.

The guerrilla struggle in Co. Kerry was particularly bitter and saw some of the worst atrocities of the war. At Ballyseedy Cross nine IRA prisoners were tied to a landmine and blown up, with eight of them killed. Four more were murdered at Countess Bridge, Killarney, and five others tied to a mine and killed at Caherciveen.

Daly's Dublin Guards earned a fearsome reputation for brutality in Co. Kerry, as did Colonel David Neligan. Neligan had been one of Collins' key intelligence officers during the Anglo-Irish War and as the head of NA intelligence in Co. Kerry was accused of torturing and executing Republican prisoners.

Sadly both sides violated the rules of war and the IRA was not above shooting unarmed civilians, using the excuse that supporters of the Treaty were effectively 'combatants'. In November an unarmed NA medical orderly, John Lydon, was shot outside Tralee, Co. Kerry and in March 1923 four NA prisoners were executed in Wexford on the orders of Bob Lambert, the local IRA commander.

The Government was astute enough to realize that coercion alone would not work and in October 1922 offered to grant an amnesty to any Irregular who signed an undertaking to abandon the struggle. Whilst some took advantage of the offer many Republicans remained in arms. They were viewed as traitors by the Government's supporters, which probably explains why NA soldiers were willing to treat them so ruthlessly.

The Republican cause was dealt a further blow when the Catholic Church recognized the pro-Treaty administration in Dublin and condemned the Republican cause. Whilst Lynch was contemptuous of politicians, writing that 'at present it is a waste of time to be thinking too much about policy', de Valera knew that some form of Republican 'Government' was essential.

Timothy Michael Healy (1855–1931), first Governor-General of the Irish Free State (1922–27) (Corbis)

De Valera argued that, as the pre-Treaty 2nd Dáil was still the legitimate government of Ireland, those of its members in arms against the Saorstát were in effect the *de jure* Irish government. Once more de Valera styled himself 'President of the Irish Republic' and appointed a 12-man Council of State consisting of Austin Stack, Robert Barton, Count Plunkett, J.J. O'Kelly, Mrs O'Callaghan, Mary MacSwiney, P.J. Ruttledge, Seán Moylan, M.P. Colivet and Seán Mahoney.

The Republican Government was virtually penniless and its members ignored by the IRA command. Consequently de Valera never really expected it to function properly but rather to provide continuity between the 2nd Dáil and what would follow a Republican victory.

The Republicans' lack of financial resources meant that looting and commandeering became a necessary means for the Republican forces to survive. According to Hart the IRA carried out over 141 armed robberies and 111 raids on the mail, and attacks on grocery and bread vans along with the destruction of bridges and railway lines did little to gain public support.

Although the Saorstát's August offensive had put the IRA on the back foot it was not beaten. Again adopting British tactics the NA conducted large cordon and search operations that resulted in the capture of several Republican leaders including O'Malley, Deasy and Moloney. It was during such an operation that Lieutenant Larry 'Scorecard' Clancey fatally wounded Lynch in the Knockmealdown Mountains, Co. Waterford on 11 April 1923.

Command passed to Aiken, who had declared for the Republican cause in August 1922. IRA activity was highest in the remote areas of the south and west; they did carry out some successful attacks on NA garrisons but rarely held on to captured towns. Instead they resorted to ambushes although few were executed with the determination of the earlier conflict.

When Deasy called from his prison cell for an 'immediate and unconditional surrender of arms' and Republican prisoners

held in Limerick, Cork and Clonmel gaols also publicly appealed for an end to the war it was obvious that the IRA was losing heart.

Although hardliners on both sides rejected calls for a truce Aiken, Barry, Collins, Dalton, Deasy, Mulcahy and de Valera had all made tentative approaches to the other side to discuss peace. In fact this may have been one of the reasons that Collins had made his ill-fated trip to Co. Cork in August 1922.

After Lynch's death in April 1923 it became increasingly obvious to the majority of Republicans that the war was unwinnable. Over 12,000 IRA were in prison along with many of their leaders. The Government's use of executions and amnesties had also taken its toll, leaving a small hardcore of guerrillas in the field. Republican Tom Crofts was convinced that 'if five men are arrested in each area we are finished'.

Despite his solid Republican credentials Aiken had never been enthusiastic about the 'armed struggle' against his former comrades-in-arms in the NA and one of his first acts as IRA Chief of Staff was to sound out his commanders' attitudes to a ceasefire. By 14 May 1923 both the Republican Government and the IRA Executive endorsed this policy and ten days later he ordered his troops to dump arms and go home.

De Valera issued a statement claiming that 'further sacrifice on your part would now be in vain and the continuance of the struggle in arms unwise in the national interest. Military victory must be allowed to rest for the moment with those who have destroyed the Republic.' To all intents and purposes the civil war was over.

Soldiers stand by a train wrecked in an IRA ambush at Cloughgordon c.1922. © Hutton-Getty Library

Major-General James Emmet Dalton MC 1898–1978

Considering that Emmet Dalton was a Secretary to the Senate, played such a prominent role in the IRA during the Anglo-Irish War, commanded the artillery that attacked the Four Courts, broke the back of the 'Munster Republic' and was with Collins when he was killed at Béal na mBláth it is astonishing that so little information about his life seems to have survived. His name crops up again and again in accounts of Ireland's revolution yet a casual search of the internet turns up very little. He left no published memoirs and except for a series of interviews for RTE no biography of Emmet Dalton has yet been written.

Born in the USA on Friday 4 March 1898, Dalton grew up at 8 Upper St Columbus Road, Drumcondra, a solidly middle-class Catholic suburb of Dublin, and was educated by the Christian Brothers at their school in North Richmond Street. The O'Connell School still survives and has an extensive museum commemorating its old boys; however, neither Dalton nor Brendan Finucane – the youngest wing commander in the RAF during World War II – receives a mention in it.

Dalton's father was a third-generation Irish-American Republican who had returned to Ireland in 1900 and his family's political activism probably explains why he joined the Dublin Volunteers at their inaugural meeting in 1913 at the tender age of 15 and was actively involved in smuggling arms by the time he was 16. His younger brother Charlie also joined and went on to become a member of Collins' inner circle.

Much to the chagrin of his father, in 1915 Dalton answered Redmond's call to arms, joining, at 17, the British Army as a temporary 2nd lieutenant in the 7th (Service) (Dublin Pals) Battalion, Royal Dublin Fusiliers (RDF). By 1916 he was attached to the 9th Battalion, RDF, 48th Infantry Brigade, 16th Irish Division under Major-General W.B. Hickie. Most of the officers and men in this Division were Redmondite Home-Rulers and like Dalton were horrified by the news of the Easter Rising.

Major General Emmet Dalton MC, Director of Operations of the National Army and architect of the Free State victory in the south-west. He was with Collins when he died. (Corbis)

It was whilst serving with the 9th 'Dubs' that Dalton befriended an old acquaintance of his father, Lieutenant Tom Kettle MP, the 36-year-old Nationalist MP for East Tyrone and Professor of Economics at University College Dublin. It was Kettle who had famously declared that Irishmen should fight 'not for England, but for small nations', a sentiment that Dalton seemed to fully endorse. Kettle hoped that, 'with the wisdom which is sown in tears and blood, this tragedy of Europe [World War I] may be and must be the prologue to the two reconciliations of which all statesmen have dreamed, the reconciliation of Protestant Ulster with Ireland, and the reconciliation of Ireland with Great Britain'.

By the summer of 1916 the 16th Irish Division were fully embroiled in the bloody battle of the Somme. On 9 September 9 RDF attacked the Germans near the village of Ginchy and Kettle, then acting as OC B Company, was shot and killed within sight of Dalton. The fighting around Ginchy was bloody and along with Kettle over 4,314 Irishmen became casualties; 1,167 of them were never to see Ireland again. It was also a battle where heroism went hand in hand with sacrifice. Dalton was amongst those recognized for their courage and was awarded the Military Cross whilst Lieutenant John Holland of the Leinsters won a Victoria Cross.

For the rest of his life Dalton was known as 'Ginchy'. According to his Military Cross citation he 'led forward to their final objective companies which had lost their officers. Later whilst consolidating his position, he found himself with one sergeant, confronted by 21 of the enemy, including an officer, who surrendered when he attacked them.' Later that year King George V presented him with his medal at Buckingham Palace. In many respects it was typical of the courage he demonstrated throughout this military career and such was his pride in the award that on occasion he even wore the ribbon on his NA uniform.

By 1917 Dalton had returned to his old battalion, 7 RDF, 30 Brigade, 10th Irish Division in Palestine where he first commanded a rifle company and then became OC of a sniping school. By 1918 what was left of 7 RDF along with A/Major Emmet Dalton MC redeployed to the Western Front. Speculation that he once served on the staff of Sir Henry Wilson is unfounded, as is the unsubstantiated innuendo that he was a British spy and shot Collins.

Like thousands of other Irish soldiers he returned to Ireland after the war. Whilst Dalton was 'away at the wars' his brother Charlie was an active Volunteer who became a member of Collins' 'Squad', his hand-picked team of assassins, and was one of the participants in the Bloody Sunday killings of 21 November 1920. It is unclear whether he used the German pistol his brother had given him as a souvenir.

It was probably inevitable, given Charlie's connections and his military experience, that Dalton rejoined the Volunteers on leaving the army. As a disillusioned Redmondite he probably felt that after the 1918 General Election the Dáil and the IRA best represented the will of the Irish people. He had fought for Ireland during World War I and once said that he had no difficulty fighting for Ireland with the British or fighting for Ireland against the British.

Regardless of his personal beliefs Dalton developed a close friendship with Collins and in an interview screened by RTE on the day he died in 1978 said, 'I loved him. I use no other word. I loved him as a man loves another man, with pure love.'

When Seán MacÈoin was captured in March 1921 it was Dalton who led the attempt to rescue him from Mountjoy Gaol. Dressed in his old uniform and leading members of Collins' 'Squad', he had devised a plan that was typically daring and involved a stolen armoured car, British Army uniforms and a lot of luck. Dalton and Joe Leonard, dressed as British officers, managed to bluff their way into the Governor's office on the pretence of moving MacÈoin to another prison before they were rumbled and shooting broke out near the prison gate. Although the rescue attempt failed Dalton managed to extract his raiding party intact.

His raw courage as well as his wealth of military experience won him the admiration and trust of both Collins and Mulcahy. His membership of Collins' inner circle was also unusual, as he does not appear to have been a member of the IRB. His loyalty to Collins was purely personal rather than doctrinal and despite his pedigree as an ex-British officer he rose rapidly through the IRA's ranks to command the Active Service Units during the failed attack on the Customs House in May 1921. In addition he became the first Director of Munitions and, by the time the Truce was agreed in July 1921, the Director of Training for the IRA.

When Collins was nominated to go to London as part of the Irish peace delegation Dalton was dismayed that the 'Big Fella' would be negotiating with the British but accompanied him nonetheless as his military advisor and head of security. He felt that the Treaty was the best deal that Ireland could get and true to his loyalty to Collins he came out in support of it.

In January 1922 Dalton became a brigadier in the new NA when his unit was absorbed into the Dublin Guards. Along with J.J. 'Ginger' O'Connell and John Prout who had both served in the US Army, Dalton was one of the few senior officers in the NA with formal military training. When Dalton's troops began shelling the Four Courts on 28 June 1922 he even helped aim and fire the borrowed British guns for their inexperienced crews.

Dalton's real *coup de main*, however, was his amphibious attack on Cork on 8 August 1922. Michael Hayes told Mulcahy that the attack broke 'all the rules of common sense and navigation and military science'. Without charts and at one point holding a gun to the head of the captain of his ship, the *Arvonia*, Dalton put ashore 456 men, an armoured car and an 18lb gun outside Cork. According to Tom Crofts 'there was panic'

People line the street in Dublin as the funeral procession of Michael Collins passes by on its way to City Hall where he lay in state before burial. 5 September 1922. (Corbis)

and, after fighting at Rochestown and Douglas, Cork fell to Dalton on the 9th, making a Saorstát victory almost inevitable. In fact Dalton complained bitterly that the war could have been brought to a close in September 1922 if troops had also attacked overland from Dublin at the same time.

On 12 August the now Major-General Dalton was appointed General Officer Commanding, Southern Command. He announced that it was his avowed aim to restore normality to the city and helped establish a temporary police force until the Garda arrived on 16 September. In late August Collins was in Co. Cork, ostensibly on an inspection tour but also attempting to make contact with leading Republicans to end the war; according to Coogan's biography of Collins, Dalton had been central to this 'peace' process and acted as an intermediary.

When Collins was warned that it was not safe for him to drive around the county he told local NA commander Joe Sweeney that, 'whatever happens, my fellow countrymen won't kill me'. When the IRA ambushed Collins' convoy on 22 August Dalton had shouted, 'Drive like hell' but Collins contradicted him. Dalton attributed Collins' death to his lack of combat experience: 'if Mick had ever been in a scrap he would have learned to stay down'.

To this day no one really knows what happened at Béal na mBláth but it was obvious that Collins' death affected Dalton. When he returned from his honeymoon in September 1922 his heart was no longer in the fight. He objected to the execution of captured Irregulars and resigned his commission in December to work briefly as the Secretary to the Senate. In a military career that had spanned eight years he had become a retired major-general at 24 on a pension of £117 per annum.

Despite being an accomplished soldier Dalton had always been interested in the cinema and by the late 1920s was working as a film producer who gained some trans-Atlantic success. In the late 1950s he helped establish the Irish Ardmore Studios where the films *The Blue Max*, *The Spy who Came in from the Cold* and *The Lion in Winter* were filmed in the 1960s.

After 1922 Dalton never held a military appointment again even though Lord Mountbatten offered him the command of an Irish special operations unit in World War II. Dalton declined, preferring to follow the 'sport of kings' – horseracing – and produce his movies. On his 80th birthday, 4 March 1978, Emmet Dalton died in Dublin, barely commemorated by the State he did so much to create.

The wider impact of the Irish Civil War

Northern Ireland

Even though the bulk of military activity during the Anglo-Irish War had taken place in south-west Ireland it was events in the north-east that precipitated the cycle of violence that led to the Truce in 1921. Ulster was unlike the rest of the country in that it was where the bulk of the Protestant population was concentrated and where the majority supported Unionism.

Unionists viewed the Government of Ireland Act as the final settlement to the Home Rule issue and consequently felt that the Anglo-Irish Treaty was nothing to do with them. It was in essence an agreement between the Catholic Nationalist South and the United Kingdom and as such the Unionist leader, Sir James Craig, refused to have any part in it.

This, of course, was a source of great irritation to Republicans who viewed all of Ireland as an indivisible unit and partition as yet another example of British divide and rule. In truth the British would have quite happily included Ulster in the deal and Lloyd George did try to persuade Craig to participate.

Craig's price for participation was recognition of Northern Ireland as a separate entity by the Dáil. Although the reality was that Ireland was already divided, few Nationalists were willing to accept this. It was certainly a price that de Valera, as President, was unwilling to pay, which guaranteed that the Northern political establishment played no active role in the Treaty negotiations.

Consequently tensions increased rather than decreased in Ulster after the Truce and

attacks on British forces in the North continued apace, leaving 19 members of the British security forces dead and 46 wounded at a cost of three dead IRA. However, after

The streets of Belleek, Co Fermanagh, shortly after the town had been recaptured and occupied by British troops supported by armoured cars. (Corbis)

fighting broke out in the South in June 1922 IRA attacks on the security forces virtually ceased. Tactically the IRA faced a very different situation in most of Ulster than in the rest of the country. Here the enemy was not just the British security forces but also a significant portion of the population.

It was because of this that Ernest Blythe TD believed that attempts to coerce the North would be counterproductive. Although Blythe was a member of the IRB and the Dáil and a Provisional Government minister he was also an Ulster Protestant, which gave him a unique insight into the Ulster Unionist mind. He also believed that as long as the South teetered on the brink of civil war, Ulster Unionists would see no merit in reunification.

That is not to say that all Ulster Unionists were content with partition. Many would have preferred to remain Irish Unionists within the United Kingdom, but this was

not a realistic option after 1921. Only the Ulster Unionists viewed the division as permanent, as both the Nationalists and the British hoped that reunification was possible; where they differed was in how it could be achieved.

Whilst both the British and Provisional Governments had publicly rejected coercing the North into a unified Irish State, behind closed doors Collins was in contact with anti-Treaty IRA leaders to plan an offensive against Northern Ireland. This offensive, in combination with the 'Belfast Boycott', would destabilize Northern Ireland,

leaving it with little alternative but to join a united Ireland.

The Northern Offensive was part of the attempt to maintain IRA unity but when it finally came it was a dismal failure. Although they were on opposite sides in the South both Collins and Lynch co-operated in planning the offensive and supplying arms to Northern IRA units. Collins had privately reassured officers of Commandant-General Charles Daly's anti-Treaty 2nd Northern Division IRA that partition would never be recognized even if it meant 'the smashing of the Treaty'.

Collins was desperate to avoid implicating the Provisional Government in IRA activity in Ulster and made sure that none of the weapons supplied could be traced back to NA sources. Unfortunately the British were well aware of Collins' involvement because Lynch had publicly complained about shortfalls in the supply of laundered weapons, which only helped to fuel the growing mistrust between pro- and anti-Treaty IRA.

Operational security was lax and it was claimed that the offensive's start date, 19 May, was common knowledge in Dundalk pubs. A pre-emptive attack on Musgrave

Street Barracks, Belfast, went wrong on 17 May, resulting in talk of aborting the offensive.

Once more contradictory orders and confusion plagued IRA activity and Roger McCorley, a Belfast IRA officer, complained that 1st and 4th Northern Divisions failed to act. Another IRA officer, Tom MacAnally, accused the 2nd Northern Division of not 'doing a damned thing'. Only the 3rd Northern Division carried out any attacks.

Any pretence that the offensive was the work of the anti-Treaty IRA was exposed when fighting broke out between the USC and pro-Treaty troops under the command of Commandant-General Joe Sweeney in Belleek on 28 May, resulting in the death of Special Constable Albert Rickerby. Sweeney's men were also engaged with the USC in Pettigo further along the Donegal–Fermanagh border.

The situation was doubly sensitive, not only because both Belleek and Pettigo straddle the border but also because Sweeney had been conducting unauthorized cross-border raids into Northern Ireland to confiscate arms. On 21 March 1922 *The Times* had already referred to a 'state of guerrilla war on the border' that the Belleek–Pettigo incident did little to dispel.

To make matters worse the British Army was drawn into the fighting and, on 4 June, after a brief bombardment that killed seven IRA and wounded six others they occupied Pettigo, taking four IRA prisoners. For the next couple of months the British Army occupied the Belleek–Pettigo area, in effect creating a buffer zone between the IRA and the USC.

Whilst it was humiliating that the British had occupied territory on their side of the border the Provisional Government felt powerless to do much about it. The offensive was dealt a further blow when over 350 Northern IRA and Sinn Féin members were rounded up and imprisoned after William Twaddell, a Belfast Unionist MP, was

Irish refugees pour into Dublin. A large number of refugees from Belfast arrived in Dublin, where they were quartered in Marlborough Hall. (Corbis)

assassinated on 22 May. In addition all Republican organizations were proclaimed illegal.

General Macready reported that 'the disorganisation caused by the action of the police since 22 May has been greater than was supposed'. IRA reports talked of demoralization and disintegration. It was a blow that would ensure that IRA activity within the 'occupied six counties' had virtually ceased to exist by the time the civil war broke out in the South.

The outbreak of civil war made the lot of the Northern IRA even more miserable, as despite their opposition to the Treaty many attempted to remain neutral. In the end Aiken reluctantly threw in his lot with the Republicans because he had been arrested by Provisional Government troops in Dundalk and when he became IRA Chief of Staff after Lynch's death he did his utmost to end hostilities.

As indicated by *The Times*, the border was a major bone of contention in Anglo-Irish affairs. The Treaty had provided for a Border Commission but the Ulster Unionists simply abstained from participation. Having already lost the three Catholic-dominated Ulster counties of Cavan, Donegal and Monaghan, Unionists were unwilling to surrender any of the remaining six. In fact Craig had famously stated that 'what we have now we hold, and we will hold against all combinations'.

To make matters worse the Provisional Government's Home Affairs Minister, Kevin O'Higgins TD, doubted whether anyone in Northern or Southern Ireland or Britain had any faith in the Commission. In the end its findings were never published and the *de facto* border was only formally recognized as part of the 1998 Good Friday Agreement.

Of course the Belleek–Pettigo crisis was not the first major incident involving the border. In January the Monaghan Gaelic football team, which included IRA Major-General Dan Hogan, had been arrested *en masse* on their way to play in the final of the Ulster championships in Londonderry. In February the IRA crossed the border and

kidnapped 42 prominent Loyalists as hostages to gain the release of the footballers.

To make matters worse a trainload of USC clashed with the IRA at Clones Station, in the South, and Craig advocated sending 5,000 men over the border to rescue the captive Loyalists. The British suspended troop evacuations and feared that open conflict was about to break out between the two Irish states. Ultimately Hogan and the others were released and the crisis passed.

Even though Collins claimed in the *Daily Mail* that his policy towards Ulster was 'not understood' he was optimistic that, despite the friction between North and South, mutual interests and economic persuasion would bring about reunification. For Collins the IRA campaign was only one element of a broader strategy.

Economic persuasion took the form of the 'Belfast Boycott', which targeted Northern Irish goods and services. As Protestants owned the majority of Northern businesses the boycott did nothing to endear the Southern State to Northern Unionists and one IRA report claimed that military action was not only 'futile and foolish' but also increased the risk of exposing the Catholic minority to sectarian violence.

Sadly sectarian violence in Ulster was rife and Hart points out that whilst the Catholics made up only 23 per cent of the Northern Ireland population they amounted to 44 per cent of the casualties and 20 per cent of refugees frp, the Six Counties. Between 1920 and 1922 over 259 Catholics and 164 Protestants died as a result of sectarian attacks. In addition over 1,000 Protestants were driven from their homes in Nationalist areas and as many again lost their jobs in the Belfast shipyards alongside Catholic colleagues for being too socialist or insufficiently Loyalist.

RIGHT 'The Gal I Left Behind Me' might be the title for this photo, snapped as the very last of the Crown forces were evacuating their barracks in Ireland, leaving Erin to start the New Year with not a single British soldier on duty in it. (Corbis)

As a consequence of sectarian violence in the north-east, Southern Protestants became extremely vulnerable to revenge attacks. Unlike their Northern co-religionists Southern Protestants had played almost no part in the Anglo-Irish War; they had no political party or paramilitaries to 'defend' their interests. By Ulster standards, sectarian violence in the South was small scale with the worst incident being the killing of 13 West Cork Protestants by anti-Treaty IRA on 26–28 April 1922.

Although both the Provisional Government and the IRA condemned these

attacks the general breakdown of law and order in rural areas ensured that both were powerless to prevent them. The net result was that the Protestant population of Southern Ireland declined, causing a minor refugee crisis in Britain during 1922, and 34 per cent of it had emigrated by 1926.

It would be wrong to imply that because of their fundamental differences politicians from North and South did not talk directly with each other; they did. In January Craig and Collins agreed the first of two pacts aimed at reconciling their differences. The pact promised to end sectarian violence and the Belfast Boycott and peacefully resolve the border issue.

Unsurprisingly it failed to deliver because of Southern unwillingness to recognize Northern Ireland and Unionist intransigence over the border. The hope had been that the two Irelands could solve their problems bilaterally without recourse to the British. Unfortunately the collapse of the pact created a situation that many felt could only be resolved by British intervention.

In March Churchill brokered a second 'Collins–Craig Pact'. Collins agreed to use his authority to end IRA activity in the North whilst Craig undertook to release political prisoners and seek the restitution of sacked Catholic dockyard workers. Although the pact boldly proclaimed that peace was declared and was welcomed by the media in both Northern and Southern Ireland it triggered a wave of sectarian violence in Belfast.

Thus, after several weeks of bitter debate, acrimonious correspondence and double dealing by both Collins and Craig, the second pact went the way of the first. It would be another 50 or so years before any attempt would be made to gain a North–South consensus on the governance of Northern Ireland.

Both pro- and anti-Treatyites opposed partition and Mulcahy had argued that carrying out all the Treaty's terms would 'ultimately unify the country and destroy the Northern Parliament'. By attacking the North the Republicans had merely fuelled Unionist intransigence and exposed the Catholic minority to further attack. The result, Hart argues, was that the gunmen on both sides became more proficient at killing unarmed civilians than each other.

Unfortunately, distracted by internal conflict, the Provisional Government was unable to influence events north of the border or offer much succour to Northern Catholics. In addition, with the Northern IRA effectively neutralized and the Southern IRA at war with itself, the Unionists were able to stabilize their position.

Thus, ironically, the internecine struggle in the South guaranteed the continued partition of Ireland, allowing Northern Ireland formally to vote to remain apart from Southern Ireland. Dominated by a Protestant population which distrusted both its southern neighbour and the British Government in Westminster, Northern Ireland was deeply divided, which merely stored up problems for future generations to solve.

Great Britain

Although the Anglo-Irish War and the Irish Civil War featured regularly in the British press and took up a significant amount of Government time and effort it would be wrong to assume that Ireland was the most important item on the British agenda. In the wake of World War I the British Empire had to deal with problems ranging from suppressing an insurgency in Iraq to readjusting to peace.

There can be little doubt that the British would have preferred that the Home Rule Bill had not been passed and that the Troubles that followed had not taken place. Conservative Party sympathy for the Ulster Unionists ensured that Britain failed to deal effectively with the threat of Unionist violence manifested in the UVF and arguably the crisis was only averted by the advent of World War I.

To compound their problems the British mishandled the aftermath of the 1916 Easter Rising, effectively converting a group of

Republican extremists on the fringe of Irish Nationalism into popular heroes at the heart of it. In addition they utterly underestimated the Republican movement and, as Professor Charles Townshend points out, failed to develop a coherent strategy for dealing with the insurgency that broke out in 1919.

Although not defeated by the IRA the British were painfully aware that they were not winning the Anglo-Irish War either. When a truce was finally agreed in July 1921 the British were determined to salvage what they could from the situation and protect their strategic interests. To that end the key issue for the British was Ireland's relationship with the Empire and the Crown.

The 1920 Government of Ireland Act had reluctantly envisaged a 'two Irelands' solution to the Home Rule question. The Protestant north-east would become Northern Ireland with its parliament in Stormont Castle, outside Belfast, whilst the rest of the country would become Southern Ireland with a parliament in Dublin. It was hoped that these parliaments would eventually merge to create a united self-governing region within the United Kingdom.

British hopes for the government of Ireland as a solution to the Troubles failed to materialize; however, during the Treaty negotiations it was obvious that Lloyd George outclassed the Irish plenipotentiaries led by Collins. By continually threatening to renew hostilities Lloyd George was able to brow beat the Irish representatives into agreeing to a settlement that was to split the Republican movement.

The Treaty went further than the 1914 Home Rule Act in that it gave Ireland limited independence and its own armed forces but fell far short of the independent Irish Republic envisaged by the Dáil and the IRA. What emerged was a British Dominion within the Empire that continued to recognize George V as its king. It also left Britain in control of key naval facilities, strategic defence and telegraph communications.

From a British perspective it would have been impossible to allow what had, rightly or wrongly, been an integral part of the United Kingdom to become an independent republic on Britain's western flank. Dominion status akin to that of Australia or Canada was as far as the British were prepared to go in 1921. Even de Valera recognized that Britain's strategic interests could not be ignored but preferred the rather vague concept of external association with the Commonwealth as a way of satisfying them.

Because the British could not countenance an Irish Republic on their doorstep they were willing to do almost anything to ensure that the Treaty was adhered to and that its Saorstát survived its traumatic creation. Although British troops began handing over their barracks to the IRA soon after the Treaty was signed they maintained a force of 5,000 men under General Sir Nevil Macready in Dublin as an insurance policy until December 1922.

The British also maintained a garrison in Northern Ireland and in theory they had control of the RUC and USC, although in reality the police answered to the Stormont Government rather than Westminster. When the IRA and USC clashed in the Belleek–Pettigo area it was the British Army who intervened to keep the two sides apart.

The British condemned any attempt to subvert the Treaty, such as de Valera's attempts to amend it in the Dáil, the de Valera–Collins election pact and prevarication about the contents of the Saorstát constitution. To apply pressure they suspended troop withdrawals, or, in the case of the Four Courts occupation, threatened to attack them themselves.

When Commandant Reginald Dunne, OC London IRA, and Joseph O'Sullivan assassinated Sir Henry Wilson in London on 22 June 1922, possibly on Collins' orders, the British chose to blame the anti-Treaty Republicans. They also chose to overlook Collins' involvement in planning IRA activity in Northern Ireland.

When open warfare finally broke out between the rival factions within the IRA the British openly supplied the Provisional

Government with arms to equip its embryonic army. By September 1921 the British had supplied over 27,400 rifles, 6,606 revolvers, 246 Lewis guns, five Vickers heavy machine guns and field artillery as well as several warplanes and gunboats.

Even though the Treaty provided for the withdrawal of British forces from Southern Ireland British intelligence officers continued to operate there. British intelligence also worked closely with their Irish counterparts in the United Kingdom. Cope even arranged for Irish agents to be given firearms permits whilst operating in Britain.

Although the British IRA cells consisted of only about 400–500 active Volunteers during the Anglo-Irish War they cost British taxpayers over £1.5m. Their activities were restricted mostly to arson attacks; however, some assassinations also took place and although casualties were low, with only six killed and 19 wounded on both sides, thousands of Irishmen and women were detained and the police and Special Branch developed significant expertise in countering the IRA.

Such was the degree of co-operation between British and Irish intelligence that Liam Lynch commented that a 'large quantity of supplies are available in England; the trouble is getting them across'. The fact that the British also retained control of issuing passports to Saorstát citizens allowed the British a high degree of control over the movements of Irishmen abroad.

Of course the British IRA was as divided over the Treaty as the rest of the organization. In fact Dunne's attack on Wilson may well have been a last-ditch attempt to maintain unity. According to Hopkinson the Treaty also effectively destroyed the Irish Self-Determination League and Sinn Féin in Britain. Overall the majority of the Diaspora in Britain and the Empire appear to have accepted the Treaty or desired to remain neutral in the ensuing split.

Lynch did attempt to reorganize his supporters and appointed Pa Murray from Cork as 'OC Britain' with the vague brief to 'take charge of London'. His efforts proved fruitless and by April 1923 Moss Twomey reported that 'the chances of operations in Britain are now negligible if not all together impossible'.

In March 1923 over 110 Republican sympathizers were arrested under Article 14b of the Emergency Powers Act 1920 on the orders of the British Home Secretary. They were deported to Ireland on British warships and detained by the Irish security forces under the Public Safety Act and the Restoration of Order in Ireland Act, which ironically was still extant despite the change in regime in Dublin.

These Acts had been intended for use during states of emergency and the House of Lords, the highest law court in the British Empire, ruled the deportations illegal. Consequently the British were forced to ask for their return and although the Irish complied in the majority of cases the civil war was virtually over and the damage had already been done. It was to prove to be the first of many Anglo-Irish extradition controversies.

Suitably distracted by events in Southern Ireland the British Government rapidly lost interest in Northern Ireland, whose internal governance passed from Westminster to Stormont. Inequalities in the 'Province' passed unnoticed in Westminster until the British Government was forced to impose direct rule on 30 March 1972 as a result of the Troubles that broke out in 1969.

The United States of America

The relationship between the United States of America and Ireland has always been perceived as close. The United States was the birthplace of the Fenian Brotherhood, an Irish Republican organization founded in the 1850s by Irish émigrés, and the IRB and Irish-American émigrés were and remain a significant source of support to the Republican movement.

During the Anglo-Irish War, de Valera had spent a year in the land of his birth trying to win support for the Republic from the US

Government. Reluctant to turn on their wartime ally, the President refused to meet him and the US Congress never went further than passing resolutions sympathizing with the Nationalist cause.

The problem that de Valera faced was that 'the Cause' in the United States was already in decline long before the Treaty. Although the Irish-American Diaspora was large only a small number were politically active. The claim by the American Association for the Recognition of the Irish Republic (AARIR) that it had over 750,000 members was probably an exaggeration.

Donal O'Callaghan TD commented that 'it was all a myth talking about 20 millions of their people in America. There have never been more than half a million in the Irish movement in America.' In addition it would be an exaggeration to claim that Irish-America was a united entity.

During his year-long stay in the USA, de Valera managed to clash with the leaders of two major Irish-American organizations, John Devoy of Clan na Gael and Daniel F. Cohalan of the 'Friends of Irish Freedom'. None of these differences helped the Republican cause in Ireland.

When the Treaty was finally agreed the majority of US newspapers and Irish-Americans welcomed it. James J. Phelan, a wealthy Boston-Irish banker, telegrammed the Lord Mayor of Dublin thanking God for peace and stating that he believed he expressed the 'feeling of all true friends of Ireland and England the World over'.

The fact that the mainstream Irish-American community appeared to be prepared to accept the outcome of the Dáil Treaty debates also placed those organizations with links to the anti-Treaty Republican movement in an awkward position. To defy mainstream opinion would inevitably undermine their credibility and support, as the demand for Irish self-determination appeared to have been satisfied.

Although Mulcahy had been disappointed by the Irish-American contribution to the war effort against the British he did not underestimate its potential. When the civil war broke out the Provisional Government requested and was granted a temporary injunction by the US Supreme Court effectively freezing Republican assets in the United States, which according to a report in *The Times* on 23 August 1922 'struck at the most sensitive part of their organisation'.

The Catholic Church, always a key player in the Irish-American community, was less than impressed with the divisions over the Treaty. Archbishop Curley of Baltimore believed that Ireland's American supporters 'have been humiliated by the present state of things' and worse still that Ireland was 'becoming a laughingstock'.

According to Hopkinson the deaths of Collins and Boland also helped depress Ireland's stock even further in America. In July 1922 the President of the AARIR, James Murray, even publicly announced that 'if the people of Ireland are bound to destroy each other and ruin their chances of freedom, it is their funeral not ours'.

Reluctantly de Valera was forced to accept that Irish issues were of little importance in US national politics and only mattered in cities like Boston or New York where significant Irish communities were concentrated. Even amongst these communities the anti-Treatyites had made little attempt to win over public opinion until well into the civil war.

When the Republicans finally set out to woo Irish-America their efforts were marred by squabbling. Seán Moylan and Mick Leahy, veterans of the Cork IRA, were dispatched as military liaison officers whilst J.J. O'Kelly and Joseph O'Doherty represented Sinn Féin. In addition Austin Stack, Mrs Muriel MacSwiney, Fr Michael O'Flanagan and Countess Markievicz also visited to fly the tricolour in the US.

Moylan described Laurence Ginnell, the Republican representative in Washington DC, as a 'damn nuisance' and de Valera wrote to O'Kelly despairing that 'there are five or six of you over there, and America is a big place. Surely it should have been possible to secure harmonious working.' In the end the divisions were so bad that

O'Kelly and Fr O'Flanagan left for Australia to raise funds there.

Irish-American contributions to the Republican war chest were disappointing compared to during the Anglo-Irish War and Moylan felt that a target of just $100,000 was realistic. He had little faith in the AARIR, which was, according to the Irish-American journalist J.C. Walsh, virtually non-existent as a result of the split in the Dáil.

Clan na Gael's leader Devoy was placed in an impossible position and inevitably the organization split into two factions. Devoy's faction, based in New York, had a degree of sympathy for the pro-Treatyites but the Provisional Government's prosecution of the war made it impossible for him to support it.

On the other hand Philadelphia-based veteran Republican Joe McGarrity and his supporters in Clan na Gael came out against the Treaty. The split came with the blessing of Boland, who always emphasized the importance of US funding, but was deeply regretted by Collins. The confusion over which Clan na Gael faction was recognized by the IRB further degraded the Irish cause in the US.

Both sides saw the USA as a key battleground in legitimizing their cause and did what they could to court Irish-American opinion. Although Irish-Americans have proven to be a constant source of support for their kin across the water, the Republicans never received official recognition from the US administration during either the Anglo-Irish War or the civil war.

When the US government finally met an Irish Government official, it was Professor Timothy Smiddy, the Provisional Government's envoy to the United States. Ultimately it was the pro-Treatyites with their electoral mandate and their democratic successors rather than Republican revolutionaries who won the battle for the hearts and minds of the US Diaspora.

Robert Erskine Childers DSO TD 1870–1922

Erskine Childers was many things, soldier, author, British civil servant, gun runner and member of the Dáil for Co. Wicklow, yet he was never really accepted by his fellow Republicans who never forgave his Anglo-Irish origins. He dedicated much of his life to the cause of Irish independence and much to the chagrin of his contemporaries became a close confidant of de Valera. Despite his holding no military appointment during the civil war both the British and Irish governments vilified Childers and claimed he was the evil genius behind the rebel war effort. Nothing could have been further from the truth, yet such was the loathing for Childers in Saorstát circles that he was executed under the provisions of the Public Safety Act.

Of Anglo-Irish Protestant stock, Childers' family was from Glendalough, Co. Wicklow, although he was born in London on 25 June 1870. His mother was Irish but his father was a distinguished English academic, Professor Robert Childers. Despite being orphaned as a child and placed in the care of an uncle in Co. Wicklow, Childers was educated in England at Haileybury College and Trinity College, Cambridge, which is why he sounded like an upper-class Englishman rather than an Irishman.

In 1895 he took a job as a clerk in the House of Commons and was an enthusiastic supporter of empire. His cousin, Hugh Childers, had been Gladstone's Chancellor of the Exchequer from 1882 to 1885 and was a supporter of Irish Home Rule and it is likely that he influenced Childers' own conversion to the Nationalist cause. When the Second Boer War broke out in 1899 Childers joined

the City Imperial Volunteers to fight in South Africa and was wounded in 1900. He was invalided out of the army and once back in Britain resumed his career as a clerk in the Commons.

On his return from the Boer War Childers discovered a taste for writing and in 1903 wrote the best selling novel *The Riddle of the Sands* which predicted war with Germany. The book was a bestseller and according to Churchill it played a key part in getting the Admiralty to open bases at Invergordon and Scapa Flow although in one of his more acerbic moments Arthur Griffith credited it with causing World War I.

Childers' literary talents went beyond that of a novelist and included factual studies of

Erskine Childers, the Anglo-Irish Republican TD for Co. Wicklow who was executed by the Provisional Government on 24 November 1922. © Hutton-Getty Library

military operations. In 1907 *The Times* commissioned him to write Volume V of its *History of the War in South Africa*. His analysis of the war criticized the British and showered praise on the Boer commandos. In 1910 he wrote a treatise on mounted warfare, *War and the Arme Blanche*, and in 1911 he published *The German Influence on the British Cavalry*. The future of mounted operations was one of the 'hot' topics in military circles before World War I and he was critical of British methods.

Childers was not only an accomplished writer but also an enthusiastic and expert yachtsman. When he visited the USA in 1903 he met and fell in love with fellow sailing enthusiast Mollie Osgood. They were married within a year and by 1905 had a son, also named Erskine. De Valera once quipped that Childers was an 'inflexible idealist' and when he became a convert to Irish Nationalism he became one of its

strongest advocates. In the finest traditions of the Anglo-Irish Childers became '*Hiberiores hibernis ipsos*' – more Irish than the Irish. In 1910 he resigned from his job in the Commons and in 1912 wrote *The Form and Purpose of Home Rule*.

But Childers was not just an intellectual Nationalist and on 26 July 1914 he sailed his yacht, *Asgard*, into Howth, Co. Dublin, carrying 900 rifles and 29,000 rounds for the National Volunteers. Despite his gunrunning Childers had not fully abandoned the British Empire in 1914 and when war came he joined the Royal Naval Volunteer Reserve as an intelligence officer. He saw action in the North Sea and the Dardanelles and was awarded the DSO for his efforts. By 1916 he was a lieutenant-commander when his anger

Members of St John's Ambulance Brigade provided much of the medical support to both sides in the Dublin fighting of 1922. © Hutton-Getty Library

at the violent suppression of the Easter Rising nudged him further down the road to Republicanism and in 1917–18 he was on the Secretariat of the Irish Convention.

By 1919, Childers was a major in the newly formed RAF and as soon as he was demobbed he made his way back to Ireland and joined Sinn Féin. He was soon appointed Director of Publicity for the first Dáil and became a close friend of both Collins and de Valera. An articulate advocate of Irish independence he represented the Irish Nationalists at the Versailles Peace Conference and in 1920 put pen to paper once more to attack British policy in 'Military Rule in Ireland'. By 1921 his zeal for the cause earned him a place in the Dáil as the member for Wicklow.

His pamphleteering continued with 'Is Ireland a Danger to England?' in which he launched a strong attack against the British Prime Minister Lloyd George and his government's policies in Ireland. Both Collins and de Valera recognized his value as a propagandist and he was made editor of *The Irish Bulletin*.

Both Childers and his cousin Robert Barton accompanied the Irish delegation to London in the winter of 1921 to negotiate a treaty. Collins was convinced that de Valera had ensured that Childers was appointed secretary to the delegation so that he could act as de Valera's eyes and ears, and made sure that he was excluded from much of the negotiations.

Childers was horrified that the Treaty finally signed by the Irish delegates in December 1921 bound Ireland to the British Empire and spoke out against it in the Dáil. He felt that the retention of the monarchy, the acceptance of partition and Dominion status were all fundamental betrayals of 'the Republic'. His exchanges with Arthur Griffith were particularly bitter and on one occasion Griffith even exclaimed, 'I will not reply to any damned Englishman in this assembly', such was his loathing for the 'disgruntled Englishman'.

Despite being as Irish as de Valera or even Patrick Pearse, Childers never shook off the perception that he was really an Englishman.

Even the British saw him as a traitor to the land of his birth and vilified him for it. When civil war came Childers sided with the Republicans, which earned him the hatred of the Saorstát Government. In effect Childers became the bogeyman behind every outrage and on 6 September 1921 the *Irish Times* reported that 'There is no doubt that Mr Childers is the chief military brain amongst the Irregulars.'

In reality Childers was the Director of Propaganda and Publicity for the Republican 'Government' and had no military status. Like de Valera he was more or less ostracized by the Republican military leaders who did not trust the 'Englishman' any more than the Free Staters did. He was temporarily an assistant editor of the *Cork Examiner* until Dalton overran Cork. After that he was effectively 'on the run' with his monocled associate David Robinson, another ex-British Army officer turned Republican who claimed that Childers was liked by everyone who met them on their travels.

According to Hopkinson in his book *Green against Green* Childers and Robinson resembled a couple of characters from a P.G. Wodehouse novel as they drifted around south-west Ireland in a horse and cart. Isolated from Dublin and ignored by the Republican military leadership, Childers began to despair of his situation. A plan to smuggle him to the Continent came to nothing and Saorstát propaganda continued to demonize this rather effete revolutionary. Childers was well aware of British and Saorstát efforts to blacken his name but what hurt him most was insinuations that he was actually a British spy all along.

Eventually de Valera summoned Childers back to Dublin to take up an appointment as the secretary to the underground Republican Government. En route he stopped off to visit his cousin Robert Barton at his childhood home, Glendalough House, Co. Wicklow, where he was arrested by NA troops. Although Childers was armed with an automatic pistol that had been a present from Collins he declined to use it for fear of injuring the ladies present in the house.

Childers was taken to Dublin and tried by a military court under the provisions of the Public Safety Act on 16 November 1922. He was charged with the illegal possession of a pistol, the very weapon that had been a gift from his friend Michael Collins. The weapon, a Spanish .32 automatic No. 10169, was eventually returned to Childers' family on 4 November 1939 by Cahir Davitt. Such was the animosity that he generated in Griffith and O'Higgins that the only possible outcome of his trial was a guilty verdict and a death sentence.

On the morning of 24 November 1922 Childers was led out of his cell in Beggars Bush Barracks, Dublin, to face his executioners. Unfortunately it was too dark at the appointed hour and tragically Childers was forced to wait until the light improved. To kill the time he chatted with the firing party and smoked. Whatever else was said about Childers he was a brave man who faced death with remarkable courage. He told the firing squad that he bore them no ill will and even joked that they should 'take a step or two forward, lads. It will be easier that way.'

When Churchill heard of Childers' arrest he commented that 'No man has done more harm or done more genuine malice or endeavoured to bring a greater curse upon the common people of Ireland than this strange being, actuated by a deadly and malignant hatred for the land of his birth.' Childers did not see his actions in this light and in a letter to his wife written before his execution wrote, 'I hope one day my good name will be cleared in England ... I die loving England and passionately praying that she may change completely and finally towards Ireland.'

To a degree Childers got his wish during the long years of de Valera's domination of Irish politics during the middle years of the 20th century, when his British-born son Erskine Hamilton Childers became a naturalized Irish citizen and served as a Fianna Fáil TD from 1938–73, rising to be Deputy Prime Minister in 1969. His career as a TD came to an end in 1973 when he was elected as the fourth President of the Republic of Ireland.

Tentative de-escalation

Once again there were parallels between the end of the civil war and the Anglo-Irish War in that no one could be sure that it was really over. Unlike the Anglo-Irish War, however, there was no truce, no negotiations no settlement; the Republicans conceded nothing, not even defeat, and Ireland remained on a war footing. The IRA's guerrillas simply dumped their weapons and went home to await the next time.

The fact that the IRA had not been defeated would come back to haunt the Irish Government for decades after the civil war. Although the NA had wrested control of Ireland's towns from the IRA in the opening weeks of the war Republican forces were still operating with impunity in many rural areas.

Almost 1,000 IRA guerrillas were still at large in the mountainous areas near Macroom and Bantry in Co. Cork although by May 1923 they had little stomach for the fight. Ever since Dalton had overrun the county the NA occupation had been fairly benign and IRA leader Tom Crofts even described their commander, Major-General David Reynolds, as 'decent for he did not want executions'.

The same was not true of the war in Kerry, where some of the worst atrocities of the war had taken place. In the end approximately 400 well-armed IRA guerrillas were engaged in a bitter game of cat and mouse with 2,000 or so government soldiers. IRA guerrillas were also active in north and west Mayo as well as along the border with Sligo and Leitrim.

Although none of these forces had been beaten in the field the constant pressure of being 'on the run' steadily wore them down. Conventional military operations became less and less common as attacks on Unionist and Saorstát sympathizers and their property increased along with looting, road trenching and destruction of railway infrastructure and engines.

Early defeats had also left the IRA in Co. Limerick and Co. Tipperary demoralized and relatively ineffective. Despite establishing both an army HQ and an underground government in Dublin there was little IRA activity of any note in the city or the county after the fighting in the summer of 1922.

In fact Co. Wexford was probably the only area in eastern Ireland where IRA activity increased rather than declined as the war progressed. When Aiken ordered his men to go home some areas of rural Wexford were firmly under IRA control. A *Times* report speculated that this was because a 'large portion of it [the NA], variously estimated, sympathised with the Republican cause'.

According to O'Halpin the IRA campaign was increasingly seen as illegitimate, lawless, undisciplined and ruthless. It is difficult to see the military logic of an IRA attack in Ballina, Co. Mayo where they 'demolished the park enclosure and released the hares'. O'Higgins was quite explicit that 'we are not engaged in a war properly so called, we are combating organised sabotage and a kind of disintegration of the social fabric'.

The Government undoubtedly exaggerated the extent to which social disorder in some areas was linked to Republicanism except in the context that the rule of law had been steadily undermined since the start of the IRA offensive against the British in 1919. In attempting to restore order the Irish Government faced similar difficulties to the British but unlike them they were willing to openly go beyond their legal powers to suppress the insurrection.

O'Higgins was no fan of the NA but accepted that it had to 'perform many duties which, strictly and technically, might be said to be those of armed peace rather than military'. He firmly advocated that 'there should be executions in every county.

The psychological effect of an execution in Dublin is very slight in Wexford, Galway or Waterford ... local executions would tend considerably to shorten the struggle.'

Rebels surrendering in O'Connell Street, Dublin. (Corbis)

The Saorstát Minister for Agriculture, Patrick J. Hogan TD, also believed that 'the people are thirsty for peace, and thirsty for strong ruthless measures ... an unusually steady, disciplined Army acting with the utmost efficiency and ruthlessness'.

Even Mulcahy had told Dalton that he could not afford to be broadminded when dealing with the IRA.

What was remarkable about the executions and illegal killings carried out by Saorstát forces was that the Irish public

seemed to accept them without much complaint. This was in stark contrast to the attitude of the public, in both Britain and Ireland, towards the executions carried out under the auspices of the previous administration in Dublin.

This was probably because the Saorstát Executive Committee constantly emphasized that they were defending the rule of law and democratic institutions against Republican disorder and even de Valera despaired at times of the IRA's lack of democratic legitimacy. Claiming a mandate from the first Dáil was all well and good but the Irish electorate had already moved on.

Even as the civil war was drawing to a close the IRA failed to grasp the significance of the Clausewitzian maxim that war is the continuation of politics by other means, issuing a statement that 'suggestions as to methods of ending the present struggle will be effectively dealt with by Government. Such questions do not concern the Army, whose duty is to prosecute the war with redoubled vigour.'

From the start they focused on waging war rather than developing a coherent strategy that went beyond destroying the Saorstát. The IRA Executive had always been lukewarm about the prospects of a negotiated peace, especially on anything other than their own terms. Throughout the conflict attempts had been made to bring both sides to the negotiating table with little success.

On 3 May 1923 Senators Andrew Jameson and James Douglas met with de Valera to discuss the possibility of peace talks but they foundered when he refused to sign a statement recognizing the Saorstát Government. De Valera claimed that he wanted 'a peace which would enable his followers to return to constitutional action' but he 'doubted whether his followers would be willing to publicly hand over arms'.

When Mary MacSwiney criticized de Valera for opening dialogue he scolded her for speaking 'as if we were dictating terms and talk ... of a military situation. There is no military situation. The situation now is that we have to shepherd the remnant of our forces out of this fight so as not to destroy whatever hope remains in the future by allowing the fight to peter out ignominiously.'

De Valera was not alone amongst leading Republicans in wanting to end the war and salvage what they could. Tom Barry was actively seeking to bring about an end to the conflict and Aiken believed that the best hope for furthering the Republican cause lay with the Sinn Féin Clubs through political rather than military action.

Unfortunately for the Republicans the Saorstát Government was unwilling to renege on the Treaty, which made a negotiated solution unlikely. With thousands of IRA guerrillas in custody and most of the country in Government hands Cosgrave, O'Higgins and Mulcahy showed no sign of letting up pressure on the IRA despite Aiken's orders to cease offensive operations.

The last executions of the civil war took place on 30 May in Tuam, Co. Galway, when Michael Murphy and Joseph O'Rourke were shot for their part in a failed armed robbery. De Valera was arrested on

15 August in Ennis, Co. Clare, during a political rally and between 13 October and 23 November 1923 possibly as many as 8,000 of the 12,000 Republican prisoners went on hunger strike.

Fortunately for the Government only two prisoners died during the strike and the Republicans failed to fully exploit its propaganda value. More alarmingly the strike showed that despite their captivity many IRA prisoners were far from demoralized. When the strike was finally abandoned not everyone was pleased with the order and one prisoner was heard to comment that 'I would rather have faced the firing squad than call it off, but there was Divisional Officers ordering their men off.'

With over £30m (over £4 billion in current terms) worth of damage done, £2m of uncollected rates in Co. Clare alone and £17m spent on the war effort, Cosgrave was far from happy with the situation he faced in June 1923. Although the Republicans had lost, the Saorstát's victory was far from clear and it would be several years before the Government felt confident enough to consider the civil war over.

A republic divided

Because the IRA had more or less ceased operations without actually admitting defeat Cosgrave's government spent the best part of a decade trying to contain the remnants of what would now be termed 'physical force' Republicanism exemplified by the modern IRA splinter groups. Most commentators agree that the 1920s were unhappy times for Ireland and when the IRA shot O'Higgins in 1927 many feared a second civil war.

Fortunately the shooting did not herald renewed violence but clearly illustrated the Republican movement's willingness to exact revenge on its enemies. The killing not only confirmed the Government's worst fears about the IRA threat to the Irish State but also acted as the catalyst for de Valera's re-engagement with constitutional politics.

The 1918 Irish General Election had given Sinn Féin enough parliamentary seats for them to credibly argue that *Dáil Éireann* was morally and legally the real seat of Irish government, rather than the Westminster Parliament. Unfortunately attempts to deal with the Saorstát Dáil in a similar fashion failed miserably and despite winning 44 seats in 1923 they were unable to drive a wedge between the Irish electorate and the pro-Treaty Government.

The 1922 and 1923 General Elections ably demonstrated that the Treaty's supporters had a stronger and more recent mandate than the Republicans. De Valera realized that Sinn Féin's policy of abstaining from the Dáil was counter-productive, merely enabling Cosgrave to entrench pro-Treaty attitudes and O'Higgins' death was the final straw that led him to leave it. The result was a new party, Fianna Fáil (Soldiers of Destiny) and as its leader de Valera went on to dominate Irish politics until his death in 1975.

De Valera was not alone in seeking an alternative force to a waning Sinn Féin.

The civil war had stymied de Valera's earlier attempts to create a new Republican party, Cumann Poblachta, but it was the creation of the pro-Treaty Cumann na nGaedhael (Society of Gaels) in March 1923 that proved that Nationalist unity was finished. By 1933 Cumann na nGaedhael had merged with the Centre Party and the Army Comrades Association (ACA) to become Fine Gael (the United Irish Party), modern Ireland's principal centre-right party.

Thus, the two political parties that dominate modern Irish politics, Fianna Fáil and Fine Gael, have their roots in the disintegration of Sinn Féin and the civil war. Consequently from the late 1920s former enemies faced each other across the floor of the Dáil ensuring that bitterness and confrontation rather than co-operation dominated Irish politics for decades after the fighting had ended. Worse still these animosities, as highlighted by Ryle Dwyer and Kingsmill Moore, passed down to their children, who often followed them into the Dáil, and have only just begun to dissipate.

Mainly because there had been no outright victory Cosgrave's government dedicated much of its time and effort to restoring law and order in a deeply divided country. The absence of an effective police presence in many areas led to a degree of lawlessness that could only be controlled by the military and the continuation of emergency legislation. In fact until the *Garda Síochána* was able to establish itself fully the NA remained responsible for policing as well as customs and excise duties.

O'Higgins was never happy with this state of affairs and along with Cosgrave was determined to reduce the NA, curb its power and re-establish civil governance. After a poor start the new Irish police, the Civic

Guards, were disarmed and reorganized in 1923 into the *Garda Síochána*. Despite a slack handful of fatalities in 1923–24 the Garda's lack of involvement in the war worked in its favour and allowed it to gain acceptance even in strongly Republican areas.

The war had cost the Irish economy money it could ill afford and Cosgrave's government spent much of the 1920s attempting to balance the books and restore its sources of income. His pro-British, Free Trade policies were unpopular with many but they brought a degree of stability to the country, creating institutions that in essence became the foundations of the modern Republic of Ireland.

Although Cosgrave's government became associated with both steady and reliable leadership as well as repressive internal security policies his ally O'Higgins, when he became Minister of External Affairs, was able to increase Ireland's autonomy within the Commonwealth. When de Valera finally became President of the Executive Council in 1932 he too realized how much leeway the Treaty actually gave Ireland to govern itself.

In 1927 the Royal and Parliamentary Titles Act changed the title of George V from that of King of the United Kingdom of Great Britain and Ireland to that of King of the United Kingdom of Great Britain and Northern Ireland and separately King of Ireland. This altered the constitutional position of the King and effectively removed the British Government's right to appoint the Governor-General and offer advice on Irish issues.

After 1927 only the Irish Government could appoint the Governor-General and advise the King on Irish affairs. A similar situation was also created in the other self-governing Dominions of Australia, Canada, New Foundland, New Zealand and South Africa, with Britain increasingly leaving them to their own devices. Unlike the rest of the Commonwealth, however, Ireland was also granted its own Great Seal, re-emphasizing its secession from the United Kingdom.

Britain's hold over its Empire was further weakened by the 1931 Statute of Westminster, which granted the 'parliaments' of self-governing Dominions equal status to the Westminster Parliament. In essence the statute removed British interference from the Dominions' internal affairs and established the principle that the United Kingdom would not block appointments or legislation passed in the Dominions even if they were 'repugnant to the law of England'.

The 1936 abdication of Edward VIII gave de Valera the opportunity to remove all reference to the monarchy from the Irish constitution. Irish voters approved a new constitution, *Bunreacht na hÉireann*, in 1937, renaming the country Éire or simply Ireland. The new constitution not only explicitly laid claim to Northern Ireland but also effectively made Ireland a republic in all but name.

Despite this sleight of hand Ireland remained a monarchy and Commonwealth member until 1949 when the Republic of Ireland Act came into force, finally

William Cosgrave, President of the Irish Free State with Kevin O'Higgins and Commander O'Reilly. (Corbis)

making the Republic a reality once more. Significantly the British did nothing to prevent it happening, so much had Britain's relationship with its Empire changed in the aftermath of World War II.

When war broke out in 1939 Ireland was the only Commonwealth country not to declare war on Germany and remained neutral throughout what was euphemistically called 'the Emergency' by the Irish. Neutrality was a central tenet of de Valera's foreign policy and, to the astonishment of many at home and abroad, he even offered his condolence to the German ambassador when he received news of Hitler's suicide.

The return of the Treaty Ports[3] in 1938 had indicated Britain's belief that even under

3. As a condition of the Anglo-Irish Treaty Britain retained the deep water ports of Berehaven, Queenstown (Cobh) and Lough Swilly as sovereign bases. Their existence was one of the factors that made anti-Treaty Republicans oppose the settlement. The ports remained under British control until the 1938 Anglo-Irish Free Trade Agreement – many Irish supporters of neutrality believed that their return was vital in the years leading up to World War II.

Irish revolutionary leader Èamon de Valera, reading from notes, addresses a huge crowd of Dubliners during his years as Prime Minister of Ireland. De Valera was among the most influential of Irish Republican leaders of the 20th century; he played a large role in creating the Irish Free State in 1922, and then in 1937 led the initiative to sever Ireland's ties to the British Commonwealth and become a sovereign state. (Corbis)

created problems for its armed forces whose preoccupation was internal security until 1958 when Ireland began to contribute to the United Nations and more recently to other international peacekeeping operations. Mulcahy had wanted to create a professional, politically neutral military that would in his own words serve 'even a de Valera Government' and in that he was largely successful.

The army that emerged 'victorious' from the civil war was, however, far from politically neutral and was deeply divided. Personal loyalties, especially to Collins, rather than belief in the Treaty, had brought many into the NA. The members of 'the Squad' were particularly problematical. They had carried out some of the least savoury operations for Collins and later as members of the Criminal Investigation Department (CID) were probably responsible for dozens of illegal killings during the civil war.

General Liam Tobin eventually became their spokesman and in January 1923 formed the 'Old IRA' to safeguard the interests of IRA veterans serving in the NA. Many of them felt that they deserved better treatment than they received but with a Government deficit of over £4m huge defence cuts were inevitable and thousands of soldiers had to be discharged.

The 'Tobinites' believed that Mulcahy favoured retaining ex-British officers and by March 1924 tensions within the army were such that the Old IRA issued an ultimatum warning that unless there was an end to demobilization and the dismissal of Mulcahy they would 'take such action that will make clear to the Irish people that we can no longer be party to the treachery that threatens to destroy the aspirations of the nation'.

de Valera Ireland would help out in any future war. Consequently the British were far from happy with Irish neutrality although in reality the Irish Government discreetly aided the Allies. Ireland was as dependent on the North Atlantic convoys as the United Kingdom for its survival and over 100,000 Irish citizens fought in the war. At least 3,000 even deserted from the Irish military to do so.

Despite Ireland's being economically and strategically linked with the UK, Irish neutrality continued after the war and

As a result 50 officers resigned their commissions and some absconded with their weapons, again leading to Government fears that they were in cahoots with the Republicans. Cosgrave's ill health gave O'Higgins the opportunity to exploit the situation and dismiss Mulcahy along with his Chief of Staff MacMahon, the adjutant general Lieutenant-General Gearóid O'Sullivan and the quartermaster general Lieutenant-General Seán O'Muirthile.

Although Mulcahy's removal had been one of the mutineers' aims the Government refused to give in to the rest of their demands and the mutiny collapsed. The 1924 Defence Forces Act finally put the Permanent Defence Force (PDF; a new name for the National Army) on a stable footing and banned its members from belonging to oath-bound organizations uch as the IRB, IRA or freemasons.

Consequently when Fianna Fáil formed a government in 1932 its fears about the army proved unfounded and de Valera was pleasantly surprised how apolitical the PDF had become. In the years that followed the mutiny the PDF was often starved of funds and neglected by successive Irish governments. Despite this it has evolved into an extremely efficient and professional force whose loyalty, quite rightly, is to the democratically elected government of Ireland, regardless of that government's politics.

Although the Tobinites had failed to restore their fortunes within the NA the collapse of the mutiny did not end their intrigues. By the end of 1925 there was significant evidence to indicate that they were involved in negotiations with the Republicans to 'act together to overthrow the government'. In the end the talks came to nothing but according to O'Halpin they afforded a rapprochement between the Tobinites and Republicans.

Such intriguing ensured that the Irish security forces expended much effort in monitoring clandestine organizations such as the IRA who posed a threat to the State. It is easy to forget that the IRA never recognized the legitimacy of the Irish State and considers its 'Army Council' as the successor to the pre-civil war Dáil and thus effectively the Provisional Government in exile of the Irish Republic. Even when de Valera came to power he did what he could to curb IRA activities in Southern Ireland.

By the 1950s 'physical force' Republicanism had become a spent force in the politics of Ireland even if the same was not true of Northern Ireland. Although partition had been one of the catalysts of the civil war it was not the central one and successive Irish governments did little to end it. The failed IRA campaign from 1956 to 1962 did nothing to improve the lot of Nationalists in Northern Ireland or weaken the resolve of Unionists to keep their Province out of a united Ireland.

The RUC had more or less neutralized the Northern IRA at the start of the civil war and kept a close eye on Republican activity within its borders. Unionists feared that the IRA was being sustained by Dublin and the presence of men like de Valera, Aiken and O'Malley in the Irish Government did little to persuade them otherwise. In reality the Irish Army and Garda deployed significant resources to interdict IRA incursions from the Republic.

When the Northern 'Troubles' broke out in 1968 the Irish Government did contemplate using the army to secure areas along the border to create 'safe havens' for Catholics displaced by sectarian violence. In the end such action became unnecessary when British troops deployed, much to the horror of the IRA, to defend Catholic enclaves from Loyalist attacks.

The IRA response was slow in coming and resulted in yet another schism in the organization when it divided into the 'Official' and the predominantly Northern 'Provisional' IRA in the early 1970s. True to Behan's quip about 'the Split' when the Provisional IRA declared a ceasefire in 1997 two splinter groups, the 'Continuity' and 'Real' IRA, emerged to briefly continue the 'armed struggle'.

In 1972 the British suspended Northern Ireland's parliament for failing to deal effectively with the Troubles and spent the next 30 years trying to end the conflict. Of course to Republicans Britain was as much a part of the problem as the Unionists and it was not until the 1998 Good Friday Agreement between Unionists and Nationalists as well as the British and Irish Governments that a solution seemed possible.

One consequence of the Good Friday Agreement is that the Republic renounced its territorial claim over Northern Ireland although its residents retain the right to Irish citizenship, thus ending one of the major stumbling blocks in Anglo-Irish relations. Despite the continuation of low-level para-military violence the declaration in 2006 by the Provisional IRA that its campaign was over was also another significant milestone.

Although the issue of partition remains as yet unresolved it appears that paramilitary violence is passing out of Northern Ireland's

politics as it has done in the Republic. Even if the scars of the civil war are still sore in some parts of Ireland they have at least begun to heal. Since the 1970s the conflict's protagonists have slipped from the stage leaving politicians with no personal experience of the war to govern.

Bitter though the civil war undoubtedly was and despite the many difficulties experienced since, Ireland has developed into a less introspective, more stable and prosperous liberal democracy playing a full and valued part in both the European Union and the United Nations. Ultimately, perhaps Collins was right all along when he claimed that the Treaty had given Ireland the 'freedom to achieve freedom'.

General Seán MacÈoin hoists the flag over Customs Barracks, Athlone, following the takeover. (Image courtesy of the National Library of Ireland)

Glossary and abbreviations

AARIR American Association for the Recognition of the Irish Republic

ASU Active Service Unit; originally part of the Dublin IRA, comprised of full-time IRA guerrillas, it later became part of the Dublin Guards. In a broader sense, the term came to mean any small, full-time IRA guerrilla unit.

Civic Guards the new constabulary established by the Saorstát in February 1922, following the departure of the Royal Irish Constabulary (RIC). In September 1922 it ceased to be an armed force and it was renamed the *Garda Síochána* in August 1923.

Clan na Gael 'Family of the Gaels'; Irish-American organization that provided the Republicans with funding and arms.

Cumann na nGaedhael 'Society of Gaels'; pro-Treaty organization founded in March 1923.

Dáil Dail Eireann, 'Assembly of Ireland'; the extralegal 'parliament' formed in 1919 by Sinn Féin MPs who refused to recognize the British Parliament. It merged with the Southern Irish Parliament in 1922.

DORA Defence of the Realm Act.

DSO Distinguished Service Order.

Fianna Fáil 'Soldiers of Destiny' party, founded in 1923 and led by Èamon de Valera. It remains today as one of Ireland's major political parties.

Military equipment being shipped to Ireland by Britain. (Corbis)

Fine Gael 'United Irish Party'; modern Ireland's principal centre-right party, created in 1933 by the merger of the pro-Treaty Cumann na nGaedhael (Society of Gaels) with the Centre Party and the Army Comrades Association (Èoin O'Duffy's fascist 'Blueshirts').

Four Courts the centre of the Irish justice system, around which fighting was based in 1916 and in the civil war.

Garda a contraction of *An Garda Síochána*; the Irish police force. It was given this name, which remains in force today, in 1923, when it replaced the Civic Guards.

GHQ General Headquarters of the IRA.

Government of Ireland Act Sometimes called the 4th Home Rule Act, this act of December 1920 provided for a Southern Irish Parliament in Dublin and a Northern Irish Parliament in Belfast to govern the Protestant North.

IPP Irish Parliamentary Party; the face of Irish Nationalism in the British Parliament between 1882 and 1918, holding the majority of Irish seats before their influence waned.

IRA Irish Republican Army.

IRB The Irish Republican Brotherhood; created in the 1850s, this organization had strong links with the Irish-American community and was a secret society dedicated to throwing off the 'yoke of Saxon tyranny' and creating an Irish Republic.

Irish Diaspora [define based on explanation to be provided in text].

Irish Volunteers Splinter group of National Volunteers who refused to fight for Britain in the Great War, staying in Ireland to press for Home Rule. Led by Èoin MacNeill.

Irregulars The name given by the Irish and British Governments to the military forces who rejected the 1921 Treaty; the men themselves continued to use the name IRA.

NA National Army; the army of the Irish Free State or Saorstát, known in Irish as *Oglaich na hÉireann* after the Volunteers. Legally formed in 1923, its creation was retrospectively dated to 21 January 1922 when its first unit, the Dublin Guards, was formed. The Provisional Government sought to portray the NA as the true inheritors of the IRA and it provided the basis for the modern Irish Army.

National Volunteers Force formed by the Nationalists to counter the Unionists' Ulster Volunteer Force (UVF).

OC Officer Commanding (IRA military rank).

PDF Permanent Defence Force; the name given to the National Army following the 1924 Defence Forces Act.

Provisional Government The Government which had been created by the 1921 Treaty to administer the Free State until a general election could be held.

PSA Public Safety Act.

RAF Royal Air Force.

RDF Royal Dublin Fusiliers.

RIC Royal Irish Constabulary; police force representing the British Government in Ireland. It was disbanded in May 1922.

RUC Royal Ulster Constabulary, formed in June 1922 to replace the Royal Irish Constabulary in Northern Ireland.

Saorstát Saorstát Éireann, the Irish Free State.

Sinn Féin Irish Nationalist Party, meaning 'ourselves alone' in Irish, founded in 1905 by Arthur Griffith, and strongly Republican by 1918. Its President from [1917–23] was Èamon de Valera, who dominated Irish politics until his death in 1975.

Taoiseach Prime Minister in Southern Ireland.

TD Teachta Dála, deputy to the Dáil. Official title for a member of the Dáil.

USC Ulster Special Constabulary, formed in 1920, also known as the 'B' Specials.

UVF Ulster Volunteer Force, established by the Protestant majority in Ulster in 1913 to resist Home Rule.

Further reading

Primary sources

Dáil debates
First Dáil, Vol. F (21/1/1919–10/5/1921)
Second Dáil, Vol. S (16/8/1921–14/9/1921)
Second Dáil, Vol. T (14/12/1921–10/1/1922)
Second Dáil, Vol. S2 (28/2/1922–8/6/1922)
Third Dáil, Vols 1–4 (9/9/1922–9/8/1923)

Secondary sources

Abbott, R., *Police Casualties in Ireland 1919–1923* (Dublin: Mercier Press, 2000)

Adair, J., *Puritans: Religion and Politics in Seventeenth Century England and America* (Stroud: Sutton Publishing Ltd, 1998)

Allen, G., *The Garda Siochána* (London: Gill and MacMillan, 1999)

Babington, A., *Military Intervention in Britain: From the Gordon Riots to the Gibraltar Incident* (London & New York: Routledge, 1991)

Barry, T., *Guerrilla Days in Ireland* (New York: Robert Reinhart Publishers, 1995)

Bartlett, T., and Jeffrey, K., eds, *A Military History of Ireland* (Cambridge: Cambridge University Press, 1996)

Bell, P.M.H., *The Origins of the Second World War in Europe*, 2nd edn, 3rd imp. (London and New York: Longman, 1998)

Bennett, R., *The Black and Tans* (Staplehurst: Spellmount Ltd, 1959; repr. 2000)

Bowyer Bell, J., *The Dynamics of Armed Struggle* (London: Frank Cass Publishers, 1998)

_____*The Secret Army* (Dublin: Poolbeg Press, 1989)

Brady, C., *Guardians of the Peace* (Dublin: Prendeville Publishing, 2000)

Breen, D., *My Fight for Freedom* (London: Anvil Books, 1964)

Carver, Field Marshal Lord M., *Britain's Army in the 20th Century* (London: Macmillan, 1998)

Coogan, T.P., *De Valera: Long Fellow, Long Shadow* (London: Arrow Books, 1993)

_____ *IRA* (London: Fontana Books, 1971; repr. 1980, 1984 & 1987)

_____ *Michael Collins* (London: Arrow Books, 1990)

Coogan, T.P. and Morrison G., *The Irish Civil War* (London: Weidenfeld and Nicholson)

Cottrell, P.J., *The Anglo-Irish War, The Troubles of 1913–22* (Oxford: Osprey, 2005)

Curtis, L., *The Cause of Ireland, from United Irishmen to Partition* (Belfast: Beyond the Pale Publications, 1994)

Curran, Joseph M., *The Birth of the Irish Free State* (Alabama University Press, 1980)

Doyle, R., *A Star Called Henry* (London: Vintage Books, 2000)

Duggan, J., *A History of the Irish Army* (Dublin: Gill and Macmillan, 1991)

Emsley, C., and Weinberger, B., eds, *Policing Western Europe: Politics, Professionalism and Public Order, 1850–1940* (London: Greenwood Press, 1991)

Falls, C., *Elizabeth's Irish Wars* (London: Constable and Company Ltd, 1996)

Fanning, Ronan, *Independent Ireland* (Dublin, 1983)

Ferguson, N., *The Pity of War* (London: Penguin Books, 1999)

Hart, P., *The IRA and its Enemies, Violence and Community in Cork 1916–1923* (Oxford: Oxford University Press, 1999)

_____ *The IRA at War 1916–1923* (Oxford: Oxford University Press, 2005)

Haythornthwaite, P.J., *The World War One Source Book* (London: Arms and Armour Press, 1994)

Herlihy, J., *The Dublin Metropolitan Police: A Short History and Genealogical Guide* (Dublin: Four Courts Press, 2001)

_____*The Royal Irish Constabulary: A Complete Alphabetical List of Officers and*

Men, 1816–1922 (Dublin: Four Courts Press, 1999)

_____*The Royal Irish Constabulary: A Short History and Genealogical Guide* (Dublin: Four Courts Press, 1997)

Hezlet, Sir A., *The B Specials, A History of the Ulster Special Constabulary* (London: Tom Stacey Ltd, 1972)

Holmes, R., *The Western Front* (London: BBC Worldwide Ltd, 1999)

Hopkinson, M., *Green against Green, The Irish Civil War* (Dublin: Gill and Macmillan Ltd, 1988)

Hough, R., *Winston and Clementine, The Triumph of the Churchills* (London: Bantam Books, 1990)

Kautt, W., and Showalter, D., *The Anglo-Irish War* (London & New York: Praeger Publishing, 1999)

Kee, R., *The Green Flag, A History of Irish Nationalism* (London: Weidenfeld and Nicolson, 1972)

Kenny, K., *Ireland and the British Empire* (Oxford: Oxford University Press, 2005)

Knox, O., *Rebels and Informers, Stirrings of Irish Independence* (London: John Murray, 1997)

McLaughlin, E., and Muncie, J., eds, *Controlling Crime* (London: Sage Publications and OU, 1996 repr. 1998)

McNiffe, L., *A History of the Garda Síochána* (Dublin: Wolfhound Press, 1997)

Neillands, R., *The Great War Generals on the Western Front 1914–1918* (London: Robinson, 1999)

Neligan, D., *The Spy in the Castle* (London: MacGibbon and Kee Ltd, 1968; repr. Dublin: Prendeville Publishing, 1999)

O'Connor, U., *The Troubles: The Struggle for Irish Freedom 1912–1922* (London: Mandarin Paperbacks, 1975)

O'Farrell, P., *Who's Who in the Irish War of Independence and Civil War 1916–23* (Dublin: Lilliput Press, 1997)

O'Halpin, E., *Defending Ireland – The Irish State and its Enemies since 1922* (Oxford: Oxford University Press, 1999)

O'Sullivan, D.J., *Irish Constabularies 1822–1922* (Dublin: Mount Eagle Publications, 1999)

Pakenham, T., *The Year of Liberty, The Great Irish Rebellion of 1798*, 2nd edn (London: Abacus, 1997)

Reilly, T., *Cromwell: An Honourable Enemy* (Dingle: Brandon, 1999)

Reiner, R., *The Politics of the Police* (Hemel Hempstead: Harvester-Wheatsheaf, 1985)

Ryan, D., *Sean Treacy and the Third Tipperary Brigade IRA* (London: Alliance Press, Tralee printed, 1945)

Ryan, M., *The Day Michael Collins was Shot* (Dublin: Poolbeg Press, 1998)

_____*The Real Chief: The Story of Liam Lynch* (Cork: Mercier Press, 2005)

_____*The Tom Barry Story* (Cork, 1982)

_____*Tom Barry, Column Commander and IRA Freedom Fighter* (Cork: Mercier Press, 2003)

Ryder, C., *The RUC 1922–2000, A Force under Fire* (London: Arrow Books, 1989; repr. 1992, 1997 & 2000)

Smith, M.L.R., *Fighting for Ireland? The Military Strategy of the Irish Republican Movement* (London & New York: Routledge, 1995)

Taylor, D., *The New Police in Nineteenth-Century England: Crime, Conflict and Control* (Manchester & New York: Manchester University Press, 1997)

Taylor, P., *Loyalists* (London: Bloomsbury, 1999)

_____*Provos: The IRA and Sinn Féin* (London: Bloomsbury, 1997)

Thompson, F.M.L., ed., *Cambridge Social History*, Vol. 3 (Cambridge: Cambridge University Press, 1990)

Townshend, C., *The British Campaign in Ireland, 1919–1921* (Oxford: Oxford University Press, 1998)

_____*Ireland* (London: Edward Arnold, 1999)

_____*Political Violence in Ireland* (Oxford: Oxford University Press, 1984)

Valiulis, M.G., *Portrait of a Revolutionary* (Dublin: Irish Academic Press, 1992)

Walsh, P.V., 'The Irish Civil War 1922–1923: A Military Study of the Conventional Phase 28 June – 11 August 1922' (paper delivered New York, 1998)

Index